Practitioner's Guide to Technology, Pedagogy, and Content Knowledge (TPACK)
Rich Media Cases of Teacher Knowledge

Edited by
Mark Hofer, Lynn Bell, and Glen L. Bull

Association for the Advancement of Computing in Education
Waynesville, NC, USA

I0203002

Book layout and design by Eliana Hofer

Practitioners Guide to Technology, Pedagogy and Content Knowledge (TPACK):

Rich Media Cases of Teacher Knowledge

(ISBN # 978-1-939797-17-9) is published by

AACE, PO Box 719, Waynesville, NC 28786, USA

E-mail: info@aace.org

©Copyright 2015 by AACE

Available at http://www.editlib.org/eBooks

Table of Contents

About the Editors

Mark Hofer is a Professor in Curriculum and Educational Technology and Associate Dean for Teacher Education and Professional Services in the School of Education at the College of William & Mary. A former high school history teacher, he teaches undergraduate, masters, and doctoral courses that address curriculum-based technology integration in K-12 schools. His research and development work focuses on TPACK-based teacher knowledge development for technology integration and efforts to promote disciplined inquiry in social studies classrooms through the use of digital technologies.

Lynn Bell has worked with the Curry School of Education's Center for Technology and Teacher Education at the University of Virginia for more than a decade. She co-edits the electronic journal Contemporary Issues in Technology and Teacher Education (www.citejournal.org) and has also co-edited three books: Teaching With Digital Images, Teaching With Digital Video, and Framing Research on Technology and Student Learning in the Content Areas.

Glen L. Bull is Professor of STEM Education in the Curry School of Education at the University of Virginia, and co-director of the Curry Center for Technology and Teacher Education. He organizes and convenes the National Technology Leadership Summit (NTLS), an invitational leadership summit that brings together the leaders of a dozen national teacher educator associations for interdisciplinary discussion across professional societies. The Practitioner's Guide to TPACK is one tangible outcome designed to advance effective use of technology in teaching that has emerged from cross-disciplinary dialog at NTLS.

About the Authors

Robert Q. Berry, III is an Associate Professor in the Curry School of Education with an appointment in Curriculum Instruction and Special Education. A former mathematics teacher, he teaches elementary and special education mathematics methods courses in the teacher education program at the University of Virginia. Additionally, he teaches graduate level mathematics education course and courses for in-service teachers seeking a mathematics specialist endorsement. His research focuses on equity issues in mathematics education, pre-and in-service teachers' mathematical knowledge for teaching, and mathematics instructional quality.

Jonathan D. Cohen is an Assistant Professor of Learning Technologies at Georgia State University. He was a secondary English language arts teacher for nine years before earning a Ph.D. in education from the Curry School of Education at the University of Virginia.

Nancee Garcia lives in Auburn, Alabama, with her husband Julio and her daughter Anasofia. She earned her bachelor's and master's degrees in mathematics education and is currently pursuing her PhD at Auburn University. Nancee has been a high school geometry and discrete math teacher for the past ten years.

Marshall A. George, Professor of English & Literacy Education and Chairperson of the Division of Curriculum and Teaching at Fordham University, is a former chair of the Conference on English Education of the National Council of Teachers of English. He taught English language arts to students in grades 7-12 for ten years and has an extensive scholarly publication record.

Judi Harris is a Professor and the Pavey Family Chair in Educational Technology in the School of Education at the College of William & Mary, where she coordinates the Curriculum and Educational Technology doctoral program and teaches graduate courses in educational technology and qualitative research methods. A former elementary-level classroom teacher and technology and mathematics specialist, Judi's research and service focus upon curriculum-based technology integration, TPACK, and instructional decision-making. She co-edits the bimonthly TPACK Newsletter, available at http://bit.ly/TPACKNewsletterArchive.

Albert ("Bert") Henry Jacoby III is a Graduate Fellow at the University of Virginia's Curry School of Education, pursuing his doctorate degree in curriculum, teaching and learning. A veteran elementary school teacher, he is interested in instructional technology, professional development, and preservice teacher education.

Raina Kim holds a Master's degree in education in curriculum and instruction from George Mason University, with a specialization in instructional design and the enhancement of learning environments through technology. She is involved in the design and development of online graduate courses and is part of a research team that studies curricular implementation and teacher training as a doctoral student at the University of Virginia's Curry School of Education.

William Kjellstrom is an Assistant Professor in the Black Hills State University School of Education in Spearfish, South Dakota. He earned his doctorate work is in instructional technology from the University of Virginia.

Matthew J. Koehler is Professor of Educational Psychology and Educational Technology at the College of Education and Michigan State University. In his research he seeks to understand the pedagogical affordances (and constraints) of newer technologies for learning, specifically in the context of the professional development of teachers, and in the design of technology-rich and innovated learning environments. His website is at http://www.matt-koehler.com/

John K. Lee is Associate Professor of Social Studies Education at North Carolina State University. His scholarly work focuses on the educational uses of the online historical resources through the Digital History and Pedagogy Project at http://dhpp.org. John was a contributing writer for the College, Career, and Civic Life (C3) Framework for Social Studies State Standards and author of Visualizing Elementary Social Studies.

Lori Mann is an associate professor at Emporia State University in Kansas where she has taught for 25 years. She holds a Ph.D. in curriculum and instruction from the University of Kansas and has held licenses as an elementary education teacher and PK-12 reading specialist. Lori teaches undergraduate and graduate courses, coordinates and supervises interns in a professional development school setting, and serves as a department coordinator for the ESU reading program and as a team leader of a preservice teacher/faculty mobile device implementation.

Punya Mishra is a Professor of Educational Technology and Educational Psychology at Michigan State University, where he also directs the Master of Arts in Educational Technology program. He is internationally recognized for his work on technology integration in teacher education as well as his research on teacher creativity. His academic and creative work can be found at http://punyamishra.com

Yash Patel is an instructional technology doctoral student in the Curry School of Education at the University of Virginia. He was trained in Chemistry and Spanish at James Madison University, from where he also received his master's degree in education. He currently teaches Chemistry and Spanish for Loudoun County Public Schools in Northern Virginia.

Melanie Shoffner is an Associate Professor of English Education at Purdue University, holding a joint appointment in the Departments of English and Curriculum & Instruction. Her research focuses on secondary English teacher preparation, examining issues of reflective practice, dispositional development, and technology integration for teaching and learning.

David A. Slykhuis is an Associate Professor of Science Education at James Madison University. He is the director of the Content Teaching Academy and co-director of the JMU Center for STEM Education and Outreach. He has recently been elected as the president for the Society of Information Technology and Teacher Education. His research interests lie at the intersection of science, technology, and student learning.

Marilyn Elaine Strutchens is the Immediate past president of the Association of Mathematics Teacher Educators and a Mildred C. Fraley Distinguished Professor of Mathematics Education in the Department of Curriculum and Teaching at Auburn University. At Auburn she serves as coordinator for the secondary mathematics education and conducts research.

Andrea L. Zellner is a former High School English and Biology teacher. She is currently a graduate student in the Educational Psychology/Educational Technology Phd program at Michigan State University. Her current research interests focus on the impact of technological tools on student learning and writing achievement.

Introduction

Mark Hofer | Lynn Bell

In 2006, Teachers College Record published an article expanding on Lee Shulman's pedagogical content knowledge construct (Mishra & Koehler, 2006). Initially coined as technological pedagogical content knowledge, this construct was described by the authors as the multifaceted and interconnected domains of knowledge teachers need so they can successfully integrate technology in their classrooms. Later relabeled as technology, pedagogy, and content knowledge (TPACK), the construct achieved what few academic frameworks have accomplished – it went viral. In the nine years that have elapsed since that publication, more than 600 scholarly papers, presentations, dissertations and book chapters have been published or presented exploring ways in which this form of teacher knowledge can be developed, measured, and deconstructed. These publications include the Handbook of Technological Pedagogical Content Knowledge (TPCK) for Educators (The AACTE Committee on Innovation and Technology, 2008), a book developed for teacher educators and researchers that explored the construct in each of the primary curriculum disciplines, as well as in-service and preservice teacher education. Increasingly, TPACK is also represented in K-12 practitioner journals (e.g., Foulger & Slykhuis, 2013), conferences (e.g., Langrall, 2011), and policy and planning documents (Harris & Hofer, 2014). Why has this particular construct had such an impact on the scholarly and practitioner community?

The TPACK construct has helped us all understand the answer to a perplexing question: Why have both novice and experienced classroom teachers been so slow to adopt technology in their instruction? From the mid-1990s until the early 2000s, the answer to this question often centered on issues of access to technology, technical training, and the constraints of the K-12 teaching environment—most especially time (e.g., Cuban, Kirkpatrick, & Peck, 2001; Hew & Brush, 2007; Zhao, Pugh, Sheldon & Byers, 2002). While these barriers undoubtedly impact classroom

1-1

technology integration, many of these issues have persisted despite one-to-one computing initiatives and an increased investment and focus upon professional development for teachers (Kopcha, 2012). The TPACK construct provides a different view of the challenge. Rather than focusing on external factors, the TPACK construct suggests that the situation may be more related to the complex form of interdependent knowledge required to integrate technology in teaching practice effectively.

Mishra and Koehler (2006) argued that teachers must draw on three forms of knowledge to help them select, plan for, and implement digital technologies in their teaching – knowledge of the curriculum content, of the range of pedagogies and instructional strategies optimally appropriate for student learning, and of the affordances and constraints of the technologies themselves. However, simply drawing on these single domains of knowledge is insufficient. Rather, teachers must understand how these domains of knowledge intersect, influence, and even transform one another before they can effectively integrate digital technologies in their teaching.

Consider an example to see how these interconnected domains of knowledge play out in classroom practice. Say a teacher wants to guide students to conduct independent research on the internment of Japanese Americans during World War II. It is necessary but insufficient for teachers to know how to identify appropriate digital archives of historical documents (content knowledge), or even how to successfully search the archive (technology knowledge) if they cannot effectively manage students in the process of conducting independent research (pedagogical knowledge). The process of student research changes when you introduce a searchable digital archive with tens of thousands of possible sources of information (technological pedagogical knowledge). And how does one accomplish this in the context of a fifth-period U.S. History class in a school in Brooklyn, New York (knowledge of the context)?

When viewed in this light, it seems clear that more is at play than can be solved simply by providing access to a set of digital technologies or attending a few afterschool in-service workshops. Enduring solutions to the challenge require more strategic knowledge development of teachers' TPACK.

This book is designed to complement the AACTE's *Handbook of TPCK for Educators*. Rather than focusing on the teacher educator/research audience, this book is designed to support preservice and novice teachers in developing their TPACK. We envision this text being used in teaching methods and educational technology courses or in professional development workshops to help preservice and novice teachers develop their own integrated knowledge for technology integration.

We have structured the book around rich media cases of actual classroom practice in each of the four primary content areas in American schools: reading/language arts/English, mathematics, science, and social studies. In each content area, we offer one case at the elementary (K-5) level and one case at the secondary level (6-12), with an extra language arts case at the middle school level.

The goal of the *TPACK Practitioners Guide* is simple—to offer exemplary cases of technology integration efforts that result in curriculum-based student learning in each of the following nine content areas and grade level contexts:

- Elementary Science
- Elementary Math
- Elementary Social Studies
- Elementary Reading
- Middle School Language Arts
- Secondary Science
- Secondary Math
- Secondary Social Studies
- Secondary English

Notice that we said "curriculum-based" student learning. We selected classroom activities that clearly demonstrate digital technologies being used in the service of learning core content. In some of the cases, a specialized technology tool was selected that has a specific and limited use within the given content area, like Geometer's Sketchpad, the estimation calculator, and the timeline tool. The latter two tools were actually developed to help students learn very targeted concepts with the content area.

In other cases, teachers put their TPACK into practice using more universal technology tools they could adapt to help students learn a concept–tools like VoiceThread, Weebly, and Movie Maker. The capabilities of these universal tools enabled students to visit places virtually they could not visit in person, view digitized historical documents they might never otherwise see, write collaboratively with their classmates, or better consolidate evidence and communicate reasoning behind new understandings.

We believe an important aspect of TPACK is knowing what students need to learn, what obstacles they may face in learning it (including typical misconceptions), and what tool or combination of tools (specialized or universal) can help them achieve the learning objective.

These cases illustrate teachers' knowledge-in-action as they applied their TPACK in their classroom practice. Teachers each revealed their thinking processes to show how they made their decisions–both in planning and in the process of teaching. Through this rich view of the cases, preservice and novice teachers can learn from these "living examples of implementation" (William & Black, 1998, p. 146) and begin to develop their own TPACK.

Why Rich Media Cases?

Teaching cases can be structured in a variety of ways. Some cases are designed to highlight obstacles or challenges. Some focus more on problem solving in terms of instructional design. The rich media cases in this book are intended to serve as exemplars (as described by Merseth, 1996) opening "windows on practice" (Hutchings, 1993, p. 11). Each case focuses on illustrating a different teacher's TPACK in her classroom context, rather than emphasizing the learning or behavior issues of a particular student. We chose to structure the book around cases of classroom practice to capture some of the complexity inherent in classroom implementation.

In each case we include a number of media elements, including short video clips, student and teacher artifacts, and links to digital tools and resources. The video footage is crucial to these cases and is used in various ways: to highlight teacher thinking, to capture salient moments of TPACK in action, and to highlight student learning. The teacher interviews add to the narrative included in the text, rather than being repetitive. The Classroom in Action and Student Work videos show real teachers and students in real classrooms engaging in unscripted instruction. The video footage was captured by amateur videographers trying to keep up with a range of activity in busy classrooms. Where sound quality is less than ideal, we include subtitles for clarity.

Each case was developed in collaboration with the classroom teacher and one or more teacher educators. The classroom teachers' voices are prominent in each case. The teacher educators add their perspective through TPACK Commentary segments at strategic points throughout each case to highlight important aspects of TPACK that preservice and novice teachers may miss. Questions are also included that invite readers to think about their own current or future classroom experiences. Each case describes a single lesson or activity that effectively integrates a digital technology tool to enhance learning, although the activity may be situated in the context of a broader unit. The cases follow this general format:

1. **Scenario**. The scenario sets up the learning problem to be solved by the classroom activity. The teacher briefly describes a learning objective that is supported by national content area standards or a particular state's standards, along with the rationale for selecting a particular technology to help students overcome misconceptions, learn the desired content or develop a targeted skill.

2. **Meet the Teacher**. This section provides a brief overview of each teacher's experience, school and classroom setting and philosophy for integrating technology in the classroom.

3. **The Activity**. The primary features of theactivity are outlined, along with its placement within a larger unit and how student learning of the content was assessed.

4. **The Technology**. In this section teachers describe the primary technologies used in the activity as well as the features of the technology that, when combined with appropriate pedagogy, might increase opportunities for students to learn the content.

5. **Classroom in Action**. Through narrative and video a few salient classroom moments are presented in which an effective teacher exemplifies ways to facilitate student learning of content with technology–that is, TPACK is demonstrated in action.

6. **StudentWork**.Samples of student work are provided that demonstrate achievement of the learning goal.

7. **Teacher Reflection**. Each case closes with teachers discussing their perceptions of how the lesson was implemented, how students interacted with the lesson, and how the lesson might be improved for even better student outcomes or adapted for students with differing abilities.

Why You Might Use the Cases in Your Teaching

We envision two primary audiences for this book: educational technology teacher educators and teaching methods teacher educators. These two groups are likely to use the book in different ways in their courses and have multiple purposes for integrating these rich media cases in coursework. In this section, we outline three primary reasons teacher educators might consider using the cases to support preservice or novice teachers in developing TPACK: (a) as exemplars of classroom technology integration, (b) as launching points for helping them consider how to plan for and manage technology in the classroom, and (c) as a means to learn about the TPACK construct directly.

Cases as Exemplars of Technology Integration. In teacher education courses, one of the perennial challenges is in helping preservice teachers move past their own experiences as students and the limited access to classroom pedagogy during their internship experiences in schools to understand the possibilities of technology in education. They often see either limited or relatively basic uses of technology tools and resources in their placements. The rich media cases in this book provide a window into real classrooms where teachers are using educational technology in powerful ways to support student learning.

If the goal is to provide preservice teachers with good examples, teacher educators can assign the cases to be considered in terms of connections with the curriculum and the selected teaching strategies. One persistent challenge with technology integration is the tendency for teachers to focus on the tools, resulting in superficial or tenuous connections with the curriculum. Because these cases demonstrate effective curriculum-based applications of technology, your students can begin to see how technology can support student learning.

Similarly, uses of technology in schools are not always well-integrated with a teacher's teaching strategies. Each of the cases in this book demonstrates robust pedagogy that is supported or enhanced in unique or substantive ways with the selected technologies. You can pair the cases with further reading or discussion around the pedagogical strategies to help preservice teachers begin to develop their ability to pair appropriate technologies with particular teaching strategies.

Cases as Launching Points for Planning and Management. Planning and implementing technology-enhanced learning experiences in the classroom introduces additional complexity compared with more traditional forms of teaching. In the planning process, teachers must consider multiple variables, including blocking the time necessary in the school's computer lab or mobile cart, managing student logins for Web-based services and tools, identifying and preparing for possible technology-related challenges, and preparing a backup plan in case they encounter difficulties related to the technology.

Similarly, additional classroom management issues can arise with technology-integrated lessons. Teachers must consider how to monitor student work effectively in the computer lab, conduct long-term projects with multiple steps, set up the student response system, and more. Because the teachers featured in these cases discuss their planning and implementation strategies in depth, readers have an opportunity not only to see how other teachers have navigated these challenges, they can consider how they might approach similar situations in their own teaching.

Cases as Evidence of TPACK. For many preservice or novice teachers, learning directly about the nuances of the TPACK framework may be unnecessary or unproductive. A deep knowledge and understanding of TPACK is dependent on rich knowledge bases in the primary domains of content, pedagogy, and technology knowledge. It may be enough for them to consider how the curriculum, teaching strategies, and technologies fit together to support student learning.

In other cases, you may want to explore the TPACK construct more fully. This may be a particular focus in graduate work – both with advanced master's degree programs and in doctoral work. These cases provide an excellent opportunity for graduate students to unpack the cases to consider the interplay of these knowledge domains in classroom practice. The TPACK commentaries embedded throughout each case can serve as a launching point for further inquiry. Students can then be challenged to develop their own TPACK teaching cases – either rich media cases like those included here or narrative cases – to demonstrate their understanding of the TPACK construct.

. . . . How to Use the Cases in Your Teaching . . . .

In terms of course session planning, we have worked with faculty members using the cases in two primary ways: as asynchronous, out-of-class work or as whole group, in-class activities. Both approaches have affordances and constraints. We briefly explore each of these two approaches in this section, recognizing that there are a number of possible permutations of how instructors can integrate these cases in coursework.

Homework. The cases can be used as homework assignments that students work through individually or in small groups. They can consider the embedded questions and share their responses via a Web-based discussion board or as a paper to be turned in. This approach works well, as students have the opportunity to revisit particular aspects of the cases, consider their responses more fully than would be possible in a class discussion, or even share their questions and ideas with their mentor teachers before responding. Used in this asynchronous way, students tend to provide quite substantive responses and engage deeply with the cases. When they either share their responses with their peers or even consider the prompts in small groups, they have the added benefit of considering alternative or divergent perspectives beyond their own. This asynchronous approach to using the cases can be a more efficient way to engage with the cases, as the bulk of the work will happen outside of class time.

In Class. The cases can also be used effectively in class as well. In this approach, the class can move through the case together as a whole group. In this approach, the instructor can stop the case at any point to capture formative assessment data (formal or informal), lead a discussion of questions (suggested questions are embedded in the cases), or help the students to make connections between aspects of the case and other course topics and concepts. The discussion can take place in a whole group context or in a think-pair-share format in which students consider responses to the prompts in small groups and then share highlights with the whole group.

A student response system can be an effective way to poll the group on key aspects of the case as a means of gauging understanding. The in-class approach can be helpful in terms of more directly guiding student thinking. If students develop misconceptions as they work through the cases asynchronously, it can be difficult to correct them after the fact. With the in-class approach, however, instructors have the opportunity to steer students in productive directions, so that they are more likely to develop the desired key understandings.

However you decide to use these cases, we hope you will find them helpful in developing the pedagogical knowledge and skills that all teachers need to prepare students for future success.

· · · · References · · · · · · · · · · · · · · ·

Cuban, L., Kirkpatrick, H., & Peck, C. (2001). High access and low use of technologies in high school classrooms: Explaining an apparent paradox. American Educational Research Journal, 38(4), 813–834.

Foulger, T., & Slykhuis, D. (2013). TPACK as a tool for teacher professional learning. Learning & Leading with Technology, 41(1), 20-22.

Harris, J., & Hofer, M. (2013, March). Got research? TPACK eNewsletter update. Paper presented at the annual conference of the Society for Information Technology and Teacher Education , New Orleans, LA.

Harris, J., & Hofer, M. (2014, March). The construct is in the eye of the beholder: School districts' appropriations and reconceptualizations of TPACK. Paper presented at the annual conference of the Society for Information Technology and Teacher Education, Jacksonville, FL.

Hew, K., & Brush, T. (2007). Integrating technology into K-12 teaching and learning: Current knowledge gaps and recommendations for future research. Educational Technology Research & Development, 55(3), 223-252.

Hutchings, P. (1993). Using cases to improve college teaching. A guide to more reflective practice. Washington, DC: American Association for Higher Education.

Kopcha, T.J. (2012). Teachers' perceptions of the barriers to technology integration and practices with technology under situated professional development. Computers in Education, 59, 1109-1121.

Langrall, R. (2011). Student-driven TPACK: Implications for development and supervision. Session presented at the International Society for Technology in Education Conference, Philadelphia, PA.

Merseth, K. (1996). Cases and case methods in teacher education. In J. Sikula (Ed.), Handbook of research on teacher education. (pp. 722-744). New York, NY: MacMillan.

Zhao, Y., Pugh, K., Sheldon, S., & Byers, J. L. (2002). Conditions for classroom technology innovations. Teachers College Record, 104(3), 482-515.

Mind the Gap: Why TPACK Case Studies?

Matthew J. Koehler | Punya Mishra | Andrea L. Zellner

One teacher eagerly uses Google Reader to support the sharing of digital articles. Another has developed hundreds of creative and engaging lessons that rely heavily on using the overhead projector. A third teacher uses an interactive white board for displaying the text of his daily lectures. Each of these scenarios features a teacher employing educational technologies in order to support learners and content area goals.

The first teacher invests time in what seems like a helpful service from Google, one that is eventually discontinued. The second teacher uses an overhead projector in an interactive way with students, despite its old-fashioned reputation. The third teacher has access to the newest and greatest in interactive white boards, only to rely on it to facilitate lectures. In even these brief scenarios, we can see how complex teaching with technology can be and that identifying the most effective and promising technologies for use in the classroom remains a challenging task for many teachers.

The challenge is made even more daunting because the technologies themselves are changing so rapidly. Not surprisingly, teachers often feel overwhelmed just learning how to use newer technologies, let alone making decisions about how best to integrate them within disciplinary and classroom contexts. The choices of tools are myriad and the lists of features seemingly endless. Choosing one tool over another and investing time in learning those tools means that teachers are constantly weighing the pros and cons of each technology. These choices are also layered on top of curricular demands and the desire to connect with pedagogically sound practice.

Teaching with technology, moreover, can feel like a risk. It can often feel safer to teach with the familiar tools, be they pencils or books. Many teachers are intimidated by the logistical challenges of managing individual students' access to computers and the Internet.

Nonetheless, teachers increasingly find themselves called upon to help facilitate students' use of technology in order to help support digital citizenship or because the technology has found its way into the classroom (through district or school initiatives). Other teachers might find themselves making the opposite argument: as tech enthusiasts, they are responding to concerns that the content area learning might suffer in the face of using new technologies or that using digital tools distracts from good pedagogy.

The technology, pedagogy, and content knowledge (TPACK) framework (Koehler & Mishra, 2009; Mishra & Koehler, 2006) has entered this conversation as one way to frame the discussion about effective teaching with technology and how best to facilitate strong educational technological practices. The TPACK framework suggests that technologies should not be understood as isolated tools that can be layered on top of existing teaching practices, but rather that teachers should consider an integration of technology, pedagogy, and content knowledge in order to design highly effective learning experiences for students.

As the TPACK framework has matured, the research has described a variety of practices by which to understand teaching with technology within the complex context of the classroom. These practices and the findings of research (which are often published in research journals or presented at academic conferences) have often not made it into the hands of classroom teachers to directly influence teaching practice. Bridging this gap between research and practice is the object of this book.

This book provides both practitioners and researchers a way to see inside the technological, pedagogical, and content area choices that teachers are making. "Cases add context to theory," as Darling-Hammond and Snyder (2000, p. 529) noted. In this chapter, we will briefly introduce the TPACK framework, discuss the value of case study, and explore what it means to be a case of TPACK and how practitioners might apply the TPACK framework to their own classroom practices.

· · · · · · · ·   What is TPACK?   · · · · · · · · · · · · · · · · · ·

In its simplest form, the TPACK framework offers a way to think about educational technology and the issues surrounding the integration of technology into effective classroom instruction. As described by Mishra and Koehler (2006), the TPACK framework suggests that teachers approach technology not as an isolated skill to be mastered, but rather as an integrated form of knowledge that is interwoven with pedagogical and content area understandings. According to this framework, good teaching requires the thoughtful integration of technological knowledge, pedagogical knowledge, and content knowledge with the goal of designing discipline-based learning experiences for students.

The theory behind the TPACK framework is based on Shulman's (1986) work describing the knowledge required for effective teaching. Shulman championed the idea that successful teachers have a specialized form of knowledge, called pedagogical content knowledge, that represents specific skills and understandings about teaching a particular subject matter or content area. In short, Shulman's (1986) work provided a way to think about how general and specific forms of content and pedagogical knowledge were important to the act of teaching. The TPACK framework extended the work by Shulman by also considering the role of technology in teaching, and how technology interacts, in both simple and complex ways, with content and pedagogy (see Figure 1).

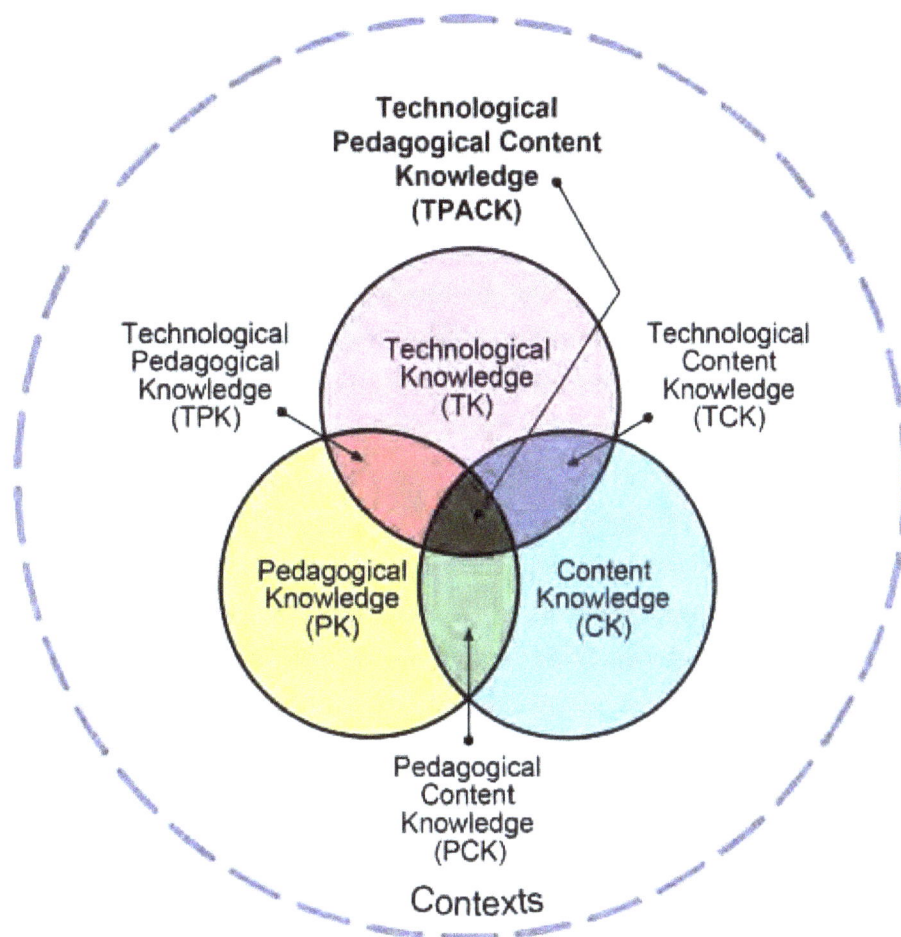

Figure 1. The components of the technological pedagogical content knowledge framework. Reproduced by permission from tpack.org

Specifically, there are three main bodies of knowledge in the TPACK framework:

* Content knowledge describes knowledge specific to the subject matter or domain for which a teacher is asked to teach.
* Pedagogical knowledge describes the teacher's understanding of best practices for teaching, various strategies, and instructional methods to support student learning.
* Technology knowledge describes the teacher's knowledge about technologies, both stable and evolving.

Additionally, the TPACK framework articulates how these three domains of knowledge interact with one another, as well as the way they might inhibit one another.

- Technological content knowledge describes the ways in which technologies and the content domain interact in ways that both impact and restrict one another. For example, reading and writing online are different than they are in traditional print, and effective literacy instruction requires an understanding of how new tools change and shape notions of literacy.
- Pedagogical content knowledge describes the ways a teacher interprets the content as both a learner and as a teacher and acknowledges that the process of engaging with content for the purpose of teaching it fosters a particular kind of knowledge. This domain includes understanding of how to teach particular topics within the broader subject matter, typical learning trajectories and misconceptions, and ways of assessing understanding.
- Technological pedagogical knowledge is a teacher's knowledge of the ways in which both teaching and learning alters with the addition of technology, especially technologies that have been repurposed for educational uses. This knowledge, for example, is demonstrated when a teacher structures online conversations differently than face-to-face discussions.
- Technological pedagogical content knowledge recognizes the deep understanding needed to weave together pedagogical, content, and technology knowledge in a way that each interacts in productive ways with the others into an act of effective teaching.

The TPACK framework itself has spawned a rich body of research into the ways teachers implement technology into their classrooms. Professional development has been designed and delivered based on this framework. Research has been conducted and published, and the larger academic discussion has shown the usefulness of TPACK as a framework for discussing these issues as well as ways to develop more practical knowledge for teachers and learners.

Despite all the work done using the TPACK framework, however, these efforts have been somewhat limited in helping classroom teachers see and understand effective uses of technology. This book represents a promising leap forward by offering concrete examples of TPACK in action, in actual classrooms, with actual students. These real-world examples serve as models to help teachers articulate the moves they make within the authentic context of the classroom that demonstrate their rich knowledge of how best to integrate technology.

Why Do We Need Cases?

Type to enter text
Case studies have a long history of use in both preservice and in-service teacher education. In general, case studies have been used as a way to highlight the contextual realities of teaching practice and to examine aspects of teaching in order to demonstrate or exemplify the complications that can arise within the classroom. Cases have been used to identify principles or concepts of a theoretical nature; to describe practice, to explore morals or ethics, to demonstrate dispositions and strategies, and also to provide an image of what is possible, among others (Schulman, 1992). Case

studies allow teachers and teacher educators to identify points of inquiry, points of tension, or points of insight. As noted:

> Typically, cases represent instances of teaching and learning that pose dilemmas, provide carefully assembled evidence or data, and, sometimes, describe the outcomes of various decisions in specific situations. Contexts for cases may be defined by the nature of the subject matter and students; the history of a class, an event, or an individual; and the situations observed or strategies attempted. (Darling-Hammond & Snyder, 2000, p. 529)

One of the greatest strengths of case studies is the manner in which they can highlight the rich telling detail, as well as local contextual factors that are often lost when teaching is discussed in more general terms.

The case study itself and its narrative structure tell the story of a moment in time in order that readers might witness what otherwise might have been invisible. When a case is studied, the reader can grapple with the decisions and choices shown in the case, as well as reflect on the outcome and imagine how different decisions might have led to different outcomes.

Case studies offer a snapshot into the complexities of the teaching context and make visible the often invisible decisions, logistics, and outcomes. The value of a case study"lies in its ability to draw attention to what can be learned from a single case (Schram, 2006, p. 107)." When taken together, as in this book, cases allow for readers to crisscross a complex domain and, thus, engage with a rich array of themes that play out differentially in different cases.

Why Do We Need TPACK Cases?

Type to enter text

The TPACK framework describes a complicated and complex set of interactions in different domains of knowledge that teachers employ when designing learning experiences with technology. Looking at specific knowledge in isolation, however, can obscure the holistic set of interactions that occur when teachers integrate technology in the classroom. TPACK cases allow the reader to see these holistic interactions in the contexts of the classrooms where the learning experiences have been designed and implemented. Considering that the classroom is already a complex and complicated context, identifying the ways that the teacher's decision making process includes choices about pedagogy, content, and technology will help readers to imagine themselves informing their own decision making process in order to support teaching and learning with technology.

TPACK cases make visible what may not be readily apparent when educational technology is used in the classroom. Not only are teachers' practices are described but teachers themselves describe the instructional and design decisions they make as they choose a particular pedagogical strategy and technology to support the teaching of particular content.

Teachers in the case studies reflect on their decisions, and the case studies offer an entry into thinking that is normally invisible during classroom observations. In focusing on the use of technology in classrooms and highlighting the ways in which the TPACK informs teaching decisions, case studies of TPACK can show the ways in which those decisions reflect the teaching context, respond to the complexity of teaching and learning, and serve as inspiration for those hoping to improve teaching with technology.

To claim that something is a case of TPACK is to say that it instantiates several important dynamics of educational technology in action. First, it provides TPACK within a specific classroom context. Every classroom is different, and the TPACK framework takes into account the ways these differences might influence pedagogical and technological decisions, as well as the type of content knowledge students are learning. Additionally, TPACK case studies highlight the ecology of decisions that led to the teaching case in three main areas, including decisions about the specifics of the school, classroom and student population, the content area goals to be addressed, and the pedagogical choices grounded in best practices of teaching. Furthermore, each case underscores the technological choices that support, enhance, or are reflective of the pedagogical and curriculum goals set for the learners. Finally, the ways in which each of these separate choices enhance and constrain one another are considered and highlighted.

The TPACK cases are also intended to serve as a place of inspiration. They invite readers to imagine how certain pedagogical methods and technologies might work within their own context.

New pedagogies or technologies often bring with them a sense of risk in terms of implementation. Whenever a new technique is undertaken in the classroom, the teacher must grapple with the newness of the approach as well as helping the students learn the content or technology or maybe both at the same time. Sometimes, students are more knowledgeable about technologies than the teacher is. Teachers assume multiple risks when trying new approaches, and this risk may create resistance toward innovation. The case study, then, allows the teacher through the narrative to experience (and simulate, so to speak, in their mind's eye) the teaching moment without the concomitant risk.

Cases of TPACK, however, are not about advocating for (or against) a particular technology. The latest and greatest technologies today can be quickly outdated tomorrow. While cases can and should serve as inspiration, they should not be seen as rigid templates for integrating technology. TPACK cases are not about recommending one technology over another, but rather about showing the thinking behind the technological choice-and how it fits with choices made regarding content and pedagogy.

Additionally, the cases presented here may or may not be representations of the best pedagogical techniques, the best content standards, the best technologies, or the best way to balance these three areas. As discussed previously, case studies are important for representing how complicated the act of teaching is. Good case studies are complicated. A reader may disagree about an approach taken in a case study discussed here. That moment of disagreement should be seen as a fruitful place to reconsider what a better approach might have been so that it might inform future practice.

TPACK cases provide an opportunity for readers to focus on concrete examples of TPACK in action and in context. They demonstrate the delicate balancing act between technology, pedagogy, and content, and how each of these enhance and constrain one another. Teachers can and do regularly pull off this balancing act, and each of the cases represented in this volume are one way to demonstrate TPACK in the real world. The cases highlight the thinking behind the decisions and actions teachers are taking, and in this way the cases can transcend a specific content area, pedagogy, and technology that might become dated over time.

Conclusion

Teaching with technology is constantly evolving even as our knowledge of effective teaching and content changes. The TPACK framework remains important despite these changes, precisely because it transcends specific content areas, pedagogies, and technologies to describe a broader approach to the question of effective teaching with technology. By itself, however, the framework may appear overly abstract and theoretical. TPACK cases provide an opportunity for teachers and researchers to engage with richly contextualized moments of teaching with technology–providing opportunities for a nuanced engagement with the framework. The case studies themselves may serve as a point of entry for those seeking to develop TPACK, or may function as examples of reflective practice. And, finally, they can serve as points of inspiration to other teachers who are seeking to improve their teaching.

References

Darling-Hammond, L., & Snyder, J. (2000). Authentic assessment of teaching in context. Teaching and Teacher Education, 16, 523-545.

Koehler, M. J., & Mishra, P. (2009). What is technological pedagogical content knowledge (TPACK)? Contemporary Issues in Technology and Teacher Education, 9(1), 60-70. Retrieved from http://www.citejournal.org/vol9/iss1/general/article1.cfm

Mishra, P., & Koehler, M. J. (2006). Technological pedagogical content knowledge: A framework for teacher knowledge. Teachers College Record, 108(6), 1017–1054.

Schram, T. (2006) Conceptualizing and proposing qualitative research (2nd ed). Upper Saddle River, NJ: Pearson Education.

Shulman, L. S. (1986). Those who understand: Knowledge growth in teaching. Educational Research, 15(2), 4-14.

Shulman, L. S. (1992). Toward a pedagogy of cases. In J. Shulman (Ed.), Case methods in teacher education (pp. 1-29). New York, NY: Teachers College Press.

Elementary Reading

Lori Mann | Erin Ardon

Interactive Activity

A balanced reading instructional approach at the early levels includes a strong emphasis on the Alphabetic Principle. The Alphabetic Principle is the understanding that words are made up of letters, and letters (symbols) represent sounds. This concept is important in early literacy development. In a nondigital environment, teachers build lessons where children have the opportunity to manipulate letters on magnetic boards as they practice early literacy skills.

Many digital applications are available for teaching letters and words to children who are beginning to read. To begin this lesson, try out the following online application called Magnetic Letters (http://www.bigbrownbear.co.uk/magneticletters/index.html) that allows practice with the digital manipulation of letters and words. Click on the following video link to learn how to use this app.

http://editlib.org/go/EL_ELA_Video1

A number of other magnetic letter applications are available for the iPad (see the Resources section at the end of this case for some alternative apps). You will see one example in this video case study. Some have a voice component with additional learning features.

? What other play with words might you be able to implement with children as part of a learning activity using the digital application Magnetic Letters?

·Scenario

Children enter school with a wide variety of experiences and skills. Some enter kindergarten as readers while others do not know how to spell their own name or identify any letters. In our diverse communities many children enter school with little or no understanding of the English language. A teacher must deal with many variables in today's classrooms, especially when it comes to literacy.

Literacy is a broad category that encompasses a wide range of areas people use in communication. In the elementary classroom, we typically think of literacy as areas in language arts such as reading, writing, spelling, speaking, and listening. The term *new literacies* has developed to help us view the world and its complex systems that make up literacy and now includes viewing and interacting with digital texts and materials. Students in today's schools must become literate in a variety of areas to function effectively in a global society and in future careers.

Balanced reading instruction is a key element in any classroom and can be delivered to a whole group, small group, or individual student. Effective teachers in the elementary classroom balance instruction by using a variety of delivery settings, groupings, and tools. Teams of teachers work together to provide the optimal learning environment for each child and his or her individual needs. Michael Pressley (2003), a key researcher and instructor in the field of literacy, wrote that three main elements play a significant role in the effective primary classroom: "a strong balance of skills with a holistic approach, over-the-top motivation, and unbelievable classroom management." Technology can support both the teacher and students by providing tools to help address these key elements.

In early elementary reading instruction students are learning basic skills that help them break the code of the letters and words and make sense of the text they see on the page or screen. They use a variety of clues, including their own prior experiences, knowledge of letters and sounds, text structure, and meaning they gain from putting together the pictures and understandable text. Basically, through the act of reading, children are learning to use problem-solving skills to make sense of the written text and the world.

The manipulation of letters and sounds in all shapes and forms is considered to be an appropriate learning activity for early literacy instruction (National Institute of Child Health and Human Development, 2000). Many tools can be used to help students work with the letters, sounds, and words that are used in reading. Children learn to identify letters, put letters together to build words, and eventually put words together to build sentences, paragraphs, and stories. Early manipulations with letters can be done through a wide variety of hands-on activities that support the kinesthetic learning needs of most children.

In the classroom you may see children working with foam letters, magnetic letters, cut-out letters, written letters, and even letters they make in the sand or form with clay. Teachers use environmental print (words posted throughout the room) to help expose children to visual representations of the letters and words. They teach children to play games, say rhymes, and sing songs to train the ear and brain to hear the patterns in the language. Exposure to printed text is deliberate, and children are saturated with experiences using text in many formats, including books and electronic devices. Electronic devices allow students extended ways to manipulate letters and sounds. They provide many opportunities for practice and application of the skills using a motivational tool they see used regularly in their surrounding environment.

In the 21st century, use of techology demands our attention. We spend much of our time with electronic devices. Think about going through your own day. You probably will spend time sending and receiving email, talking on the phone, texting messages, creating and consuming information on a variety of Internet-connected devices, communicating or collaborating using a social app like Facebook, and you may end your day by watching television.

Our children are watching this! Have you ever seen a young toddler with electronics in the room? You will quickly see the persistence the child will use to get to the device. This same interest is evident in the classroom when children are introduced to current electronic tools, especially those they have seen used by adults. Socio-cultural exposure to a world saturated with electronics is a key factor that sparks our children's interest in learning with electronic tools. Motivation is the natural result and a powerful component in education.

In this rich media case, you will get to know an elementary teacher and watch as she delivers focused small-group reading lessons to students in her primary classroom. You will see how she infuses technology into her lessons. Although the lessons here include only one or two students, components from these sessions are often delivered to an even larger group of students.

? What technologies have you used today that required you to apply your reading, writing, listening, speaking, or viewing skills? How might you use some of these same digital tools in a classroom to help students develop their own literacy skills?

Meet the Teacher

- Erin Ardon
- Title I Reading Teacher
- Lansing Elementary School

Lansing is a community with a population over 11,000 in a metropolitan area in Kansas. The Lansing Public School District serves approximately 2,600 students in grades K-12, living in the city and surrounding rural areas. My role in the school is to work with young students who are struggling with some aspect of reading while in kindergarten through second grade. I serve as a Title I/Reading Recovery teacher and work with individuals and small groups of students and assist classroom teachers. Title I is a federally funded assistance program for students needing extra assistance with math and reading. Reading Recovery is an intense early literacy program provided by highly trained teachers and developed by Marie Clay, a leader in the field of early literacy development.

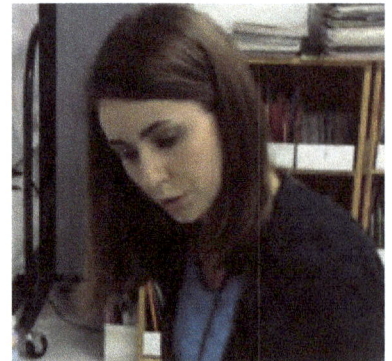

I believe the most important part of teaching children how to read and write is having an understanding that children are each different and have their own unique ways of learning. Teachers should have a solid understanding of how their students learn best and design literacy instruction which will be most effective for students. Also, continually observing and assessing student progress should aid in how their learning is structured. I believe that instruction should reflect best practices that are based in research and have proven to be effective in terms of student growth.

Watch the video to hear more of Erin's beliefs about reading instruction (http://editlib.org/go/EL_ELA_Video2).

http://editlib.org/go/EL_ELA_Video2

Incorporating technology such as iPads into traditional classroom literacy learning can have a powerful impact on children's motivation and engagement with reading and writing. When my students get to use the iPads during lessons they are excited and interested in the task, whether they are making words using a magnetic letter app, reading a digital story on a leveled-reader app, or using a drawing app to write letters and words.

The Lesson – Focus on Instruction

In this rich media case, you will see me working with my small groups during the day. We dig deeper into a lesson created to help a first grade student, Lee, become a proficient reader and writer. I also highlight my usage of technology within the small group reading time.

Highly effective teachers value small group instruction and spend more time teaching students in these settings (Lipson & Wixson, 2012) and use technology to support their instruction. I have started incorporating technology in my small-group lessons to provide additional motivation and support to the early developing readers.

Each portion of the small group lesson has been designed to address my students' instructional or just-right reading level and focuses on the following three objectives:
- The student will demonstrate an understanding of letter/sound relationships.
- The student will be able to segment sounds and work with spelling patterns.
- The student will be able to demonstrate comprehension of text through problem solving with print in a meaningful way so that decoding is purposeful and oral reading is fluent.

These general objectives are common to most early reading small-group instructional sessions. There are many formats for conducting a small group lesson, with some of the best structures remaining simple, yet balanced in the inclusion of basic literacy elements.

During each small group session, I move through many short, focused activities. I typically include the following literacy elements: familiar reads with a text we have read before, word work with magnetic letters, a writing time using a journal page, work with a cut-up sentence written by the student, an evaluation through a running record, and an introduction of a new text. I take detailed notes to help me monitor student progress and make appropriate instructional decisions. I like to offer my students experiences with both printed text and electronic text in preparation for real world activities.

In this video Erin describes more information about small group reading lessons (http://editlib.org/go/EL_ELA_Video3).

The Lesson – Focus on Organization and Assessment

As I teach, I am flexible and make adjustments to my plans to best meet the individual needs of each student; this is called differentiating instruction. To plan and record lesson notes, I use a Lesson Recording Page. Here is the Lesson Recording Page I completed before, during, and after (BDA) Lee's intense 30-minute lesson. Teachers of reading often build lessons

http://editlib.org/go/EL_ELA_Video3

using a BDA framework for planning. With my intense, longer lessons with a single child, I use this front and back one-page planning and note-taking system.

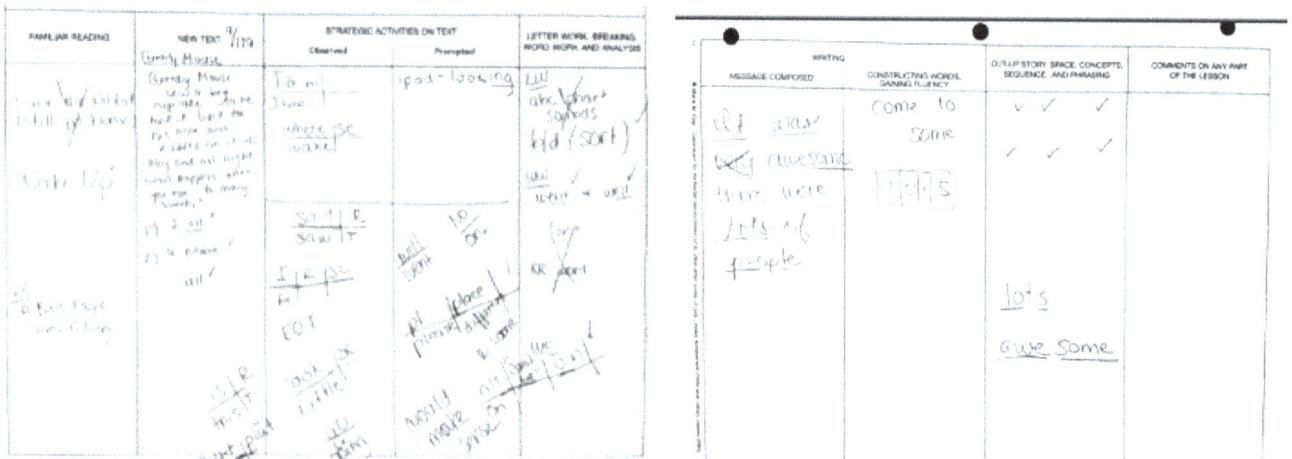

Lee works with me individually, but also works in a small group with other children. Some small groups are set up to provide direct teacher assistance, such as the Guided Reading group, and others allow students to work independently or collaboratively on specific skills or tasks. My one-on-one time provides Lee with extra attention designed specifically for his needs and allows me to keep my focus completely on him.

I try to make my lesson planning simple and organized. Although my plans are brief, preservice and novice teachers will need more detailed plans as they learn to think through all the steps involved in a lesson. I developed a short guided reading plan as a follow-up to the lesson you will watch me teach to Lee. This plan is a bit more detailed: http://editlib.org/go/EL_ELA_reading_lesson.pdf.

Later, as you watch Lee's lesson, you will notice how my plan connects and builds upon his demonstrated strengths and yet still address his needs. This small group lesson plan is framed in a BDA format, and students have the option of using the iPad for the word work and writing components. When available, I like to intersperse leveled e-books with actual paper copies.

While I work with an individual or small groups of students, the other children in the room work in Literacy Centers, stations where children work independently on previously introduced skills. Most small group instruction uses a rotational system to allow the teacher to see all students on a regular basis, with students of greatest need spending more time with a teacher and often a reading specialist. Literacy Centers allow the teacher to have uninterrupted time for direct instruction. A typical simple rotation schedule for organizing the literacy instructional time around Guided Reading groups and literacy centers might look like the schedule on the right.

Classroom Small Group Schedule

	Green	Red	Purple	Blue
8:30–8:50	Guided Reading Group	Silent or Partner Reading	Word Work at iPad Table	Writing Center
8:55–9:15	Writing Center	Guided Reading Group	Silent or Partner Reading	Word Work at iPad Table
9:20–9:40	Word Work at iPad Table	Writing Center	Guided Reading Group	Silent or Partner Reading
9:45–10:05	Silent or Partner Reading	Word Work at iPad Table	Writing Center	Guided Reading Group

When used appropriately, technology helps to keep students focused on the learning activity. I have carefully set up my room, centers, and schedule to give me easy visibility and access to my students. I have preset my iPads with only the appropriate apps needed for the task at hand. Before I begin new center activities, I assure that all my students understand how to use an app properly and understand our objective for learning. I teach my students to problem-solve and work responsibly with the iPads and with each other. Students self-monitor and know the routines of moving through activities and centers.

TPACK Commentary: Effective use of technology requires students to demonstrate ethical and self-monitoring behaviors. Teachers must guide students and cultivate an atmosphere of safety and wise decision-making, This goal can be accomplished by using a gradual release of responsibility model and proven techniques for building a community of learners.

Students in primary grades often respond well to being part of the rule-making process and need ongoing guided practice with the rules. At the beginning of the year, time should be allotted for the creation, discussion and practice of a few simple rules. Many classrooms find a pledge or classroom constitution beneficial. Role-play scenarios can be used to help students think critically about technology usage while simultaneously providing practice of communication skills critical in language and literacy development.

Effective instruction is guided by informed decisions based on ongoing assessments (Vacca et al., 2015). I am constantly evaluating my students as they read and use data to make informed planning decisions (i.e., through formative assessment). I make notes during and after each session in student portfolio files that allow me to review each child's progress and share important information with other teachers and parents. My assessments are purposeful and organized and include both electronic and paper files.

Why might it be helpful to utilize technology in small group learning time?

Time management and organization are key elements in all instructional settings. What steps could a teacher take to assure that technology usage flows smoothly during small group instruction time?

The Technology

Mobile devices are becoming popular in school settings and have the potential to change the structuring of educational settings (Magana & Marzano, 2014) and the way students learn (Collins & Halverson, 2009, p. 5). Many schools are in the midst of one-to-one, one-to-two or shared classroom-set initiatives. In these settings, children use their devices as tools, much like pencils and paper, but with more sophistication and opportunities for expanded learning. Teachers also use the devices to organize, plan, monitor, and evaluate student work. In the educational digital learning report for Kansas (Kansas State Department of Education, 2014), the setting for this case, 49% of 210 districts reported being in a one-to-one initiative of some kind, a number that is rapidly increasing every year.

The technology utilized in this case study includes an iPad. Erin's classroom contains enough devices for her students to work on them individually, although you will also notice she shares the device, at times, with her students. She has a learning table that is equipped with iPads and headsets. In another area, iPads may be used on a carpeted area in the reading corner. Erin uses all these settings and devices to support small-group instruction during individual direct instruction and paralleling literacy center time.

One application that is loaded on the iPads for the students in Erin's classroom is ABC Magnetic Alphabet (https://itunes.apple.com/us/app/abc-magnetic-alphabet-hd-learn/id379404787?mt=8), an application similar to the one you tried at the beginning of this case. This application allows children to manipulate letters to build words and analyze spelling patterns. In Erin's classroom, students use magnetic letters on a daily basis. Students alternate between the use of the ABC Magnetic Alphabet electronic application and actual magnetic letters on magnetic boards.

In his study of touch screen devices, Leon Lenchner (2009) discussed the positive effects of tools like magnetic letters in literacy instruction. By using electronic devices with a magnetic letter application, students can practice the important manipulation of letters and sounds, a simple substitution of the electronic tool for the non-electronic practice. Planning time is simplified, as the tool is easily located and ready for use with a variety of choices in applications. Magnetic Letters can provide the student and teacher with a highly interactive method of communication as they problem-solve with letter and word combinations. Follow-up with independent practice is easy and fun for children.

In apps where a voice pronounces the letter or word, instant feedback is given to the student who is working independently. Screen views can be captured through printed copies and screenshots that can be shared or saved in the portfolio. Student progress and understanding is easily captured as the student shares work with the teacher or another more skilled reader. If devices are available at home, this application makes a great tool for additional practice with parents and older siblings. All of these factors contribute to motivation and active, engaged learning. Motivation is one of the most powerful cases for using electronic devices and applications like Magnetic Letters for literacy development.

In this video, Erin talks more about the apps she likes to use to help students in their literacy learning. - http://editlib.org/go/EL_ELA_Video4.

http://editlib.org/go/EL_ELA_Video4

TPACK Commentary: Effective instruction using technology blends together content knowledge, pedagogy, and technology. In this case using the application Magnetic Letters, the content we want our students to learn is related to learning to read through practice with the manipulation of letters (content knowledge), we are applying our knowledge of effective teaching strategies and organization for small group instruction (pedagogy), and we are utilizing the iPad as our mobile device tool (technology).

Classroom in Action

In this section, you will see a series of video clips taken from Erin's work with small groups. The first clip shows Erin working with Lee near the end of his 30-minute session on a Familiar Read, his third read of this particular story. She followed up this instructional reading time with word work using the magnetic letter application on the mobile device. Remember that at this age a student's attention span is short, so the entire lesson was divided into many short activities with lots of practice reading instructional-level, or just-right, text. Look for techniques Erin used to encourage and assist Lee in his learning and observe the things she did to make the lesson flow smoothly.

Video Case: Focus on Instruction

Watch Lee's Lesson, Part 1 - Familiar Read and Magnetic Letters

http://editlib.org/go/EL_ELA_Video5

? Lee had recently learned the word *look* and demonstrated he now recognized the word while he was reading. How did Erin use technology and what she saw in this *Familiar Read* to expand Lee's learning of the word *look*?

Did you notice how smoothly Erin transitioned from the reading activity to Magnetic Letters on the mobile device? How do you think her preparations for the lesson have contributed to this smooth transition?

TPACK Commentary: The flow of the lesson you just viewed demonstrates TPACK in action. The technology was ready, available with ease, and motivational to the student. Erin's preparation included matching the right application to the lesson objective, allotting sufficient time, and considering the student's preferences and needs.

In this lesson you could observe several important teaching methodologies, that is, the pedagogy. Erin prepared the teaching environment to include all materials in a distraction-free environment (note the iPad was set up with the application ahead of time). She set the stage through a familiar routine known by the student (he jumped right into his book), allowing Lee enough wait time to think and process difficult information and providing support through questioning and help with difficult words.

Erin used a controlled vocabulary, both in context during the familiar read and in isolation as Lee practiced and expanded his knowledge of the word look on the iPad using Magnetic Letters. These activities allowed the student to decode tough words, learn new word endings, practice already known sight words, and interact with the text using comprehension skills.

Video Case: Focus on Organization and Assessment

http://editlib.org/go/EL_ELA_Video6

These next clips are a continuation of the previous lesson with Lee. Note how Erin evaluated Lee using the same iPad he just used and an app called Record of Reading. This application allows the teacher to make an auditory recording of a student's oral reading while using special coding to note miscues or errors made by the student.

Watch Lee's Lesson Part 2 - Comprehension.

? How did the iPad support Erin's assessment of Lee's literacy skills and progress during his small group instruction?

Why is ongoing assessment a key element of this lesson?

TPACK Commentary: Although this story is one Lee had read before, it was a little less familiar since he had read it only once. Did you notice that Erin used what she learned from Lee's current lesson to once again guide what they would do in another short follow-up with word work? Erin patiently gave Lee time to think and supported him with a quick return to the difficult spots to assure proper identification of the words he missed and his comprehension of the text.

Successful classrooms are organized around learning experiences that integrate assessment and instruction on a regular, ongoing basis. These experiences are not randomly happening, but carefully crafted to allow each student to progress though targeted practice and exploration. In the last video clip, you saw how Erin used technology by recording the student's voice as he read and by taking notes about his progress and miscues (or errors). The technique of recording audio and making notes with a coding system are methods commonly used as an assessment tool by teachers of reading. These recordings can be used by the teacher to plan future lessons by allowing the teacher to reexamine which objectives and standards have been met and those needing more attention. The audio recording can also be used by the student to practice and self-assess, another means of gaining more understanding.

Video Case: Literacy Centers - Independent Practice on the Mobile Device

Erin incorporated Literacy Centers with other students in the room during her session with Lee and other small groups. In this clip you will see Sean and Eddie working at their own table with words they have learned on the iPad, while Karen and Jana work at a center as a follow-up to their previous small group reading lesson.

The girls were using apps on their iPads and paper with colored pencils. They were rereading their leveled stories on their iPads and creating their own written text and illustrations to expand upon the previously discussed stories and illustrations. In some cases children in this center wrote parallel stories or created questions and answers from their own wonderings as they read.

http://editlib.org/go/EL_ELA_Video7

Many applications are available to support the writing process of elementary students, with writing being a research-based activity used to develop reading skills. In both Literacy Centers, time was used to reinforce learning that had taken place during the small group lesson and gave students a chance to collaborate as they increased their skill level.

?

What other activities might you have Lee do during his independent practice time with his own mobile device and the magnetic letter application?

Can you think of other ways a teacher might use a mobile device in this lesson and in the Literacy Centers?

Mobile devices do have the potential to access inappropriate sites and materials for the desired learning experience. How can teachers set up safe environments for students who are working independently in center environments with mobile devices?

TPACK Commentary: Using technology requires careful planning and management to assure that children are working on task and in a safe environment at all times. The goal in our educational settings is to provide a rich learning environment while protecting students in the classroom. Teachers must guide each student to develop a self-monitoring responsible learning behavior in the world, now and in the future.

In the classroom, this means developing management systems to teach responsibility and having consequences for inappropriate behaviors. Children are taught about "stranger danger" in their daily world and must also be taught about threats of a similar kind available through technology.

TPACK Commentary (continued): On-task behavior should be encouraged while still allowing children the freedom to explore appropriately. This practice can even be accomplished successfully at a young age and can lead to better habits as children move into adolescence and adulthood.

Think about your own on-task behaviors and usage of the Internet. Are you on-task in your classes? Does the Internet pose a threat to you? Do you stray away from lectures and find yourself in your email or other less desirable sites? Does this off-task behavior distract from your own personal learning or waste your time?

Preventive training under the guidance of a responsible teacher can help students learn to develop good habits and make proper decisions toward safety and best learning practices. School districts often monitor the types of sites available to students, teachers set up internal preselected applications and sites, and classrooms function under a set of technology learning responsibilities and expectations as part of the training process. These can be appropriate actions, yet for appropriate lifelong behaviors, the focus must remain on building good technology citizens through self-monitoring and the development of ethical attitudes.

Student Work

It is important to maintain files of student work for review, evaluation, and progress monitoring. Often these are kept in a student file or a portfolio, an organized collection of student work. I keep a journal of each child's writing and display student work in my room. I share the work with parents and other teachers. When done to demonstrate growth, this can be very motivational to students and gives value to their efforts. Here are some of the works created by my students during the small group lesson time and writing center time.

Lee's Small Group Lesson

This is a screenshot of two of the words we worked with during magnetic letter time. I was able to take this screenshot by holding down on the Power Button and the Home Key on my iPad. Lee struggled with the word *look* in a previous story and was just beginning to identify it in the story you watched him read on the video. I chose to have Lee practice this word he had learned and expand his knowledge by working with alternate word endings using "s" and "ing." This activity allowed him to connect sounds and letters as he spelled the word, and it prepared him for alternate forms of the base word look.

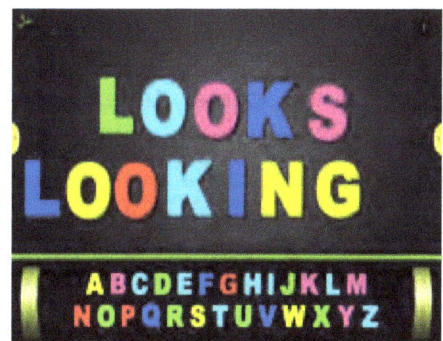

This screenshot was taken of the first page of the running record (Clay, 1993) I made of Lee reading using the Record of Reading app (http://recordofreading.com/). The check marks stand for words he said correctly while the written-out diagrams show me his errors, called miscues, and self-corrections. The columns on the right of the page can be filled out later as I analyze and tally Lee's miscues. I can save this record in my iPad and email or share it with other teachers as we collaborate on our plans for Lee's lessons.

Literacy Center Time

The students enjoyed working together in literacy center time. I do occasionally step in and help someone or refocus attention. The following work came from the time we spent in small group practicing skills we had previously learned.

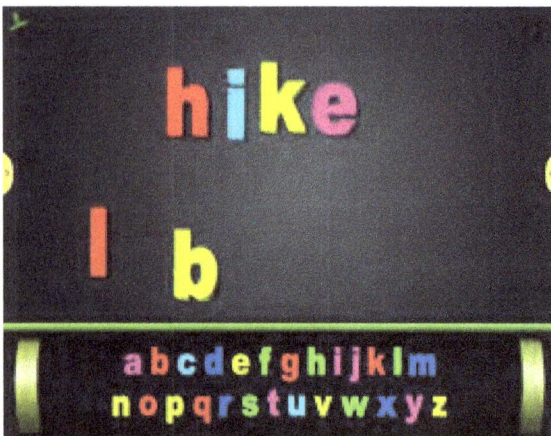

Sean's Magnetic Letters

Eddie's Letter Check

This image was taken at a point where I was providing assistance. Sean and Eddie were both trying to spell the word *like*. After they had done this, Eddie noticed his word didn't look like Sean's by comparing their screens. The two determined Sean had the correct spelling, and Eddie was able to recognize this right away.

Karen and Jana worked hard during their center time. Here you see the leveled text on Karen's iPad. Jana was using both paper and her iPad to work on her reading and writing activities.

Teacher Reflection

Reflection is important to me in my teaching. As I reflect back over the past year and this lesson, I feel very positive. The majority of my lessons with Lee went well, and he was usually focused and motivated throughout each session. The iPad aided in Lee's learning in this lesson, as he retained good focus and motivation while he used the device. My formative assessment process was infused with technology and allowed me to record Lee's reading and make informed decisions quickly and accurately as I reviewed his work on the spot. This practice saved me some time in calculating his scores, and I was easily able to share his work with other teachers.

I can also see how I have learned and grown as a user of technology. With each new endeavor or application, things seem to get a bit easier, and my lessons come together more seamlessly. By practicing with the apps and the device, my skill level is improving and I am becoming quicker with the set-up and use of the tool. I can see my knowledge base growing and am able to find better ways to help my students learn with the technology as a supportive tool. For me, the learning process is a rewarding part of my goal of continued lifelong learning as an educator.

http://editlib.org/go/EL_ELA_Video8

I am always looking for ways to improve my teaching. When I reflect back upon my lesson with Lee, I believe I might change one thing in my use of the Magnetic Letter app. I would let Lee have more control of the task. For example, he could pull up the letters to make the word instead of me doing it for him. Of course this is a case-by-case situation that will depend on the student's current abilities. Primarily, I want my students to work toward independence, so I will strive to gradually release more control to the student when using the app, just as I do with other learning processes. Lee is now ready to begin sounding out the words as he pulls up the letters.

Overall, I enjoy using the iPads as a tool in my teaching, and my students like to use them.

Resources

Clay, M. (1993). *An observation survey of early American literacy acheivement*. Portsmouth, NH: Heinemann.

Collins, A., & Halverson, R. (2009). Rethinking education in the age of technology: The digital revolution and schooling in America. New York, NY: Teachers College Press.

Kansas State Department of Education. (2014, March). *Digital learning 2014*. Retrieved from http://www.ksde.org/Portals/0/IT/TAKE/KsDL2014.pdf

Lenchner, L. (2009). *Teaching emerging literacy skills: Using touch screen technology and reading recovery inspired methods*. Retrieved from the SMART Technologies website: http://downloads01.smarttech.com/media/research/international_research/canada/smart_sympodium_dt770_ll.pdf

Lipson, M., & Wixson, K. (2012). *Assessment of reading and writing difficulties: An interactive approach* (5th ed.). Upper Saddle River, NJ: Pearson.

Magano, S., & Marzano, R. J. (2014). *Enhancing the art and science of teaching with technology*. Bloomington, IN: Marzano Research Laboratory.

National Institute of Child Health and Human Development. (2000). Teaching children to read: An evidence-based assessment of the scientific research literature on reading and its implications for reading instruction: Reports of the National Reading Panel subgroups (NIH Publication No. 00-4754). Washington, DC: U.S. Government Printing Office.

Pressly, M. (2003, Fall). Research by Michael Pressley yields insights into the practices of effective educators. *New Educator*. Retrieved from http://www.educ.msu.edu/neweducator/fall03/pressley.htm

Vacca, J., Vacca, R., Gove, M., Burkey, L., Lenhart, L., & McKeon, C. (2012). *Reading and learning to read* (9th ed.). Upper Saddle River, NJ: Pearson.

Applications for Magnetic Letters

iPad Apps - available in iTunes
ABC Magnetic Alphabet Lite (free)
Magnetic Board (free)
Magnetic Letters ($.99)
Magnetic Letters (free)
Magnet Letters (free)

Web-based Apps
Magnetic Letters   http://www.bigbrownbear.co.uk/magneticletters/index.html

Erin's Other Favorite iPad Apps

A-Z Leveled Books
Record of Reading (running record assessment)
Running Record Calculator
Who Can Read
MeeGenius

Middle School English Language Arts

Albert Jacoby | Melanie Shoffner | Marshall George | Jen Graham Wright

Interactive Activity

As you begin to consider this lesson on writing to specific audiences, watch the following video that retells an excerpt from the classic tale, "The Three Little Pigs."

http://editlib.org/go/MS_ELA_Video1

Who is the intended audience for this segment of the story? It was hard to tell, right? At first, it seemed like a story for young children. Fifteen seconds into the story, an obvious shift occurred. What changed? What can you infer about the intended audience for the second half of the story?

The ability to tailor a text to a specific audience is a hallmark of skilled writers. A clear vision of audience guides the writer's decisions about diction, syntax, rhetorical appeals, and the quantity of background information necessary to communicate ideas.

In intermediate grades, even when students are appropriately considering audience, their ability to control their language by manipulating sentence structure, syntax, diction, and other rhetorical techniques is still emerging. Students may recognize, for example, that their intended audience will be influenced by a more colloquial and familiar tone that appeals to their emotions, but may not yet have sufficient writing ability to achieve the desired effect.

The Anchor Standards of the Common Core State Standards (CCSS, 2014) state that "a key purpose of writing is to communicate clearly to an external, sometimes unfamiliar audience." The centrality of audience to the writing process is reflected in the mention of writing for an audience in virtually each year's writing standards of the CCSS.

The National Council of Teachers of English (NCTE, 2007b) supports the centrality of audience in the composition process as well, going so far as including it in their very definition of writing: "The act of writing is accomplished through a process in which the writer imagines the audience, sets goals, develops ideas, produces notes, drafts, and a revised text, and edits to meet the audience's expectations." Further, the NCTE (2007a) position paper "Beliefs about the Teaching of Writing" lists among the central goals of writing classrooms that "students should become comfortable with… strategies for preparing products for public audiences."

Often a starting point in the classroom is to have students envision an audience of their choice, then analyze that audience, identifying factors such as the audience's reading level, knowledge of the content, and for persuasive pieces, the types of arguments most likely to appeal to the audience. Traditionally, the teacher is an important arbiter of the students' work and is usually the only audience reading student-generated texts, with the occasional exception of classroom peers. However, if students are to develop and demonstrate flexibility in their writing, having access to authentic audiences who can provide feedback is important. Additionally, research shows that the presence of an authentic audience can provide students with added motivation to write and may improve the quality of students' writing.

As noted in the CCSS (2014) for writing, students can "use technology, including the Internet, to produce and publish writing and to interact and collaborate with others" (CCSS.ELA-Literacy.CCRA.W.6). Easy-to-use digital technologies afford teachers of English language arts two major ways to promote students' development in targeting their texts to specific audiences.

1. Multimedia software allows students to create rich, multimodal texts, in which images, soundtrack, and narration can share the storytelling burden with the writing. A medium like digital storytelling–a genre in which images, a narration, and a soundtrack take much of the responsibility off of the script to tell the entire story–can provide opportunities for students to hone their abilities to reach a particular audience while they continue to work on developing their traditional writing skills.

2. Web 2.0 technologies enable young writers to make connections with an authentic audience and provide them with a means of reaching their intended audience. In addition, when students share their digital writing with a real audience, they can receive feedback on the success of their writing from that very audience.

> **?**
>
> How might you help your students develop a sense of audience in their writing?
>
> What specific technology tools are you familiar with that might help students achieve this learning objective?

· · · Meet the Teacher · · · · · · · · · · · · · · · ·

- Jen Graham Wright
- 6th Grade Language Arts Teacher
- Walton Middle School

My class featured in this case study had more females than males, which is not typical of the school in general. Of the 23 students in the class, there was a mix of student ability levels, ranging from students identified as academically gifted to those with identified learning disabilities. I believe this lesson is appropriate for all students throughout the intermediate grades (4-6). Brian Kayser, a sixth-grade special education inclusion teacher, assisted me with this activity. (Watch the video for more about Jen's philosophy about language arts teaching.)

http://editlib.org/go/MS_ELA_Video2

Our school has implemented a 1-to-1 technology initiative that provides students with constant and immediate digital access through personal netbooks. All students are issued netbooks, which they take with them to class and can take home in the evenings. These devices provide students with the necessary access to many web-based tools so that they may explore and become familiar with them outside of class. This allows us to spend more class time on content, as the students are fairly competent with basic technological skills. (Watch the video for more about Jen's philosophy of technology integration in her classroom.)

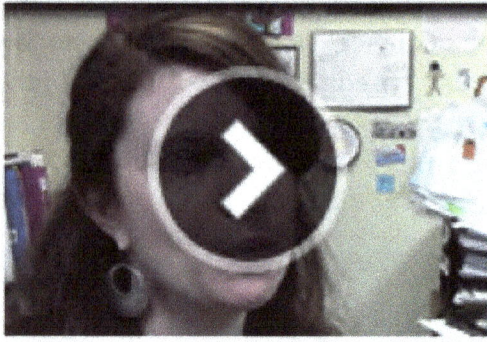

http://editlib.org/go/MS_ELA_Video3

This is my third year working with the 1-to-1 netbook initiative, and I have realized that it is not as important for students to learn how to use one particular website or program as it is to learn how to solve problems with technology. One of the problems that I want them to explore with technology is the best way to demonstrate their learning, which also forces them to think more about the purpose of the texts they are producing.

.The Activity

Introduction

Students often expect the only audience for their writing to be their teacher. In their experience, they turn in a paper and get a grade, and that is the end of it. Yet, when students realize that they have an audience beyond the four walls of their classroom, they often want to step up their game. They want to do well, not only to please the teacher, but because they know that other people are going to be looking at their work.

This activity was the culmination of a unit on fictional writing and audience. In an introductory activity on audience, students listened as I read two different versions of "The Three Little Pigs." One version of the story was standard and traditional, the other more abstract and deviating from the original plot line. Students compared and contrasted the two stories, and I challenged them to think beyond the obvious superficial differences and analyze how each story was written for a different audience.

TPACK Commentary: Teachers are aware that their students' capacity is often surpassed by their creativity. Writing can be enhanced by the technology so help students catch up with their imaginations. For example, students may want to create an eerie mood in a text, but they may lack sufficient control over syntax or have inadequate vocabularies to do so. Teachers may model these writing strategies in class, and using multimedia allows students the opportunity to practice reaching an audience as they also work in other ways to increase their traditional writing skills.

Activity

The students worked in small groups to create a digital story tailored to an intended audience—primary elementary students and students their own age. Along with the syntactic structure and vocabulary of the writing itself, students had to consider the use of imagery and a musical score to accompany their composition in the production of a digital story. I worked with the students to guide them through the steps of the writing process.

Instead of grouping students by ability level, I encouraged them to work to their strengths. They self-selected a role in which they felt they could contribute successfully to the group; writer, editor, artist, computer user, and so on. I then grouped students who could collaborate on this project. Although all students worked together in the group to contribute to each step, students each took a leadership role in their strength area.

http://editlib.org/go/MS_ELA_Video4

Working in their groups, students wrote their version of the Three Little Pigs and created visuals. In considering their intended audience, students made decisions based on vocabulary level, sentence complexity, style of artwork, and the realism of the characters' portrayals. One group even drew a character with ketchup spilled on his shirt to indicate his laziness!

After compositions underwent sufficient self, peer, and teacher review, students moved into the phase of the lesson where they worked to present their story to the intended audience. Students used school scanners to convert their images into digital formats. These images were uploaded into the digital storytelling program of choice for the group, which in most cases was VoiceThread.

Student groups then recorded their narrations directly to VoiceThread, using the built-in microphones on their computers. I guided them to focus on their fluency while reading with expression for their intended audience. The technology afforded unlimited attempts to record an acceptable version of their stories.

? What classroom management concerns might you need to prepare for when doing this type of project?

At which stages might technology play the most significant role?

What capabilities are provided by the technologies utilized?

Conclusion

Once students finished creating their digital stories, it was time for them to share. I exported the VoiceThread videos to YouTube and compiled them into lists based on their intended audiences. I emailed links to the videos to teachers of other classes of their target audiences. For the younger grades, classes watched the videos together and came up with group feedback for the authors. In the older grades, some teachers allowed students to provide individual feedback, while others chose the same method as the primary classes.

I discussed the feedback with my class to arrive at a consensus regarding each groups' success at appealing to its intended audiences. While some student groups experienced more positive feedback and success than other groups, all groups benefited from the valuable experience of receiving feedback from their intended audience.

Students were assessed based on a rubric (http://bit.ly/storyrubric) that was given to them at the beginning of the lesson. Grades were determined based on the writing and artwork being appropriate for the chosen audience. In addition to the quality of the work submitted, students were also assessed on how well they collaborated within their group and fulfilled their leadership roles in each group.

TPACK Commentary: Jen was aware that her own feedback might not help her students write effectively for their intended audience. In order to understand how writing changes for a specific audience, her student authors needed to connect to that audience in some way. Jen also understood that technology adds another dimension to the writing process. By engaging her students in digital storytelling and video sharing, she allowed them to work with a test audience prior to the final publication of their work. As students used different types of technology during the composing process, Jen was able to provide guidance and ask questions that supported their understanding of the writing process and multimodality.

The Technology

One tool Jen chose to use for this project was VoiceThread, a software application developed for collaborative presentations and available by free registration at VoiceThread.com. VoiceThread allowed students to use their own artwork and record their own voices. Jen believed it was more appropriate for presenting the stories to younger children, because it would be narrated. On the other hand, this medium required more oral reading fluency of her students, as well as more attention to expression and word choice.

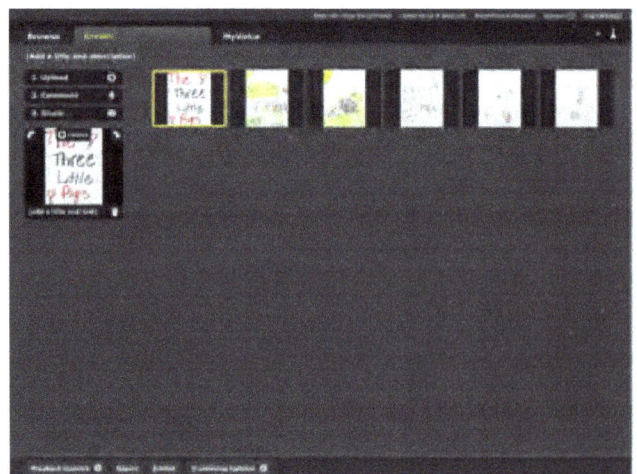

VoiceThread has a variety of annotation features and allows students to share their stories in several ways – by direct linking or embedding or by exporting to YouTube. The first two options require viewers to have their own VoiceThread account.

In this case, students elected to share their videos through YouTube. As the premiere video sharing site on the web, YouTube allows viewers to comment and rate a video as "thumbs up" or "thumbs down." YouTube also keeps track of the number of times a video is viewed, offering video owners another measure of their video's popularity. By sharing their videos and distributing a link to students in their target audience, students were able to reach out to their audience for feedback. Technology helped students reach that audience in an efficient and effective way.

Jen also gave students the option to use eBooks, which could be shared with a broader audience than a printed book could. This option required more editing work for a polished written piece, but students could still attach music and images that could impact tone or mood for an older audience.

ISTE NETS-S

According to the International Society for Technology in Education (ISTE), students must be able to learn and explore their world through the use of technology. The lesson that follows aligns with the following *ISTE National Educational Technology Standards for Students (NETS-S)*:

- **Creativity and Innovation**: Students demonstrate creative thinking, construct knowledge, and develop innovative products and processes using technology.
- **Communication and Collaboration**: Students use digital media and environments to communicate and work collaboratively, including at a distance, to support individual learning and contribute to the learning of others.

? What newer or better technology tools are you aware of that might be available for a project like this?

Classroom in Action

Throughout the portion of the unit where students worked to transform their traditional paper-pencil stories into a digital storytelling product, Jen worked with students to encourage them, keep them on task, and troubleshoot technical issues that arose.

Vignette 1

? What instructions would you give students before they begin recording their narrations?

Watch this video to see how Jen coaches her students on recording strategies.

http://editlib.org/go/MS_ELA_Video5

TPACK Commentary: The pedagogy that Jen employed was a think-aloud, where students orally justified their choices to her, allowing students to think through their choices as a group and consider how they might best reach their intended audience. Through the use of the students' personal classroom laptops, Jen encouraged the illustrator in this group to research ideas on the Internet to help him create drawings more appropriate for his intended audience.

Vignette 2

? What are some ways you might help students narrate their stories with more expression?

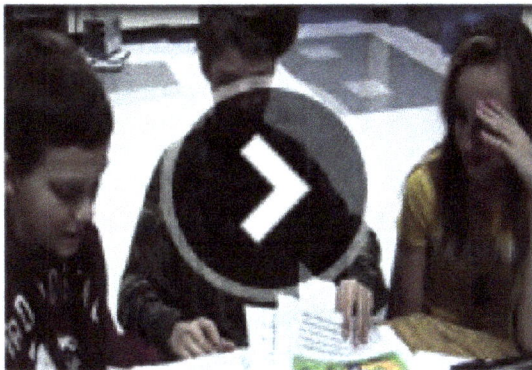

In this video, consider Jen's rapport with her students and how she encourages more expressiveness in their reading.

http://editlib.org/go/MS_ELA_Video6

TPACK Commentary: This interaction shows students struggling with their objective – reaching their target audience. Jen drew upon her pedagogical understanding to ask questions and provide information that would scaffold her students' understanding of audience. First, she asked her students to think about their own experiences of having a story read to them; next, she reminded them that their experiences could guide them in creating their story. Finally, she assured them that the technology allowed them to improve upon their mistakes during this publishing phase of the writing process..

Vignette 3

In this video, notice Jen's questioning techniques as she leads student reflection on their story and the way they considered audience.

http://editlib.org/go/MS_ELA_Video7

TPACK Commentary: Jen's choice to provide direct instruction allowed her to teach her students about certain nuances of the VoiceThread program. For example, she reminded them not to speak to one another while recording. Jen understood that an audience does not want to hear background conversations, and kindergarteners would be too easily distracted by extra sounds. Jen chose to provide this information directly to her students rather than engage them in scaffolded questioning in order to protect her students' time during the composing process. The technology itself allowed students to easily revise their work but Jen recognized the finite resource of class time to create these stories.

Student Work

Students began this project knowing the basic elements of the plot for the story that they would write. Students worked creatively with their groups in creating their own script of the familiar tale—the dialog and details, as well as the images. Students took ownership of the story and considered their audience throughout the process. In the third vignette, students selected vocabulary that they considered to be more advanced and also pushed the boundaries of their imagination in creating their images. The drawings below show the details that these students included in their project.

The wolf attacks

No more troublesome wolf

http://editlib.org/go/MS_ELA_Video8

The students in the first and second vignettes lacked the artistic ability to create their own drawings, so they sought help from the web. Using images from Kids-Pages.com, this group retold their story of The Three Little Pigs to a kindergarten audience. Believing that many kindergarteners would be unfamiliar with the original story, they chose not to deviate much from the traditional version. They selected basic vocabulary and cartoon-style artwork to tell their tale. After uploading their images and text to VoiceThread, they recorded themselves reading their script.

In this video, you will notice that the students were keenly aware of their audience and considered the audience during creation of their artwork in great detail. The students were clearly proud of the work that they created.

http://editlib.org/go/MS_ELA_Video9

The following comments on YouTube were made by kindergarten students after watching the "Three Little Pigs" video above.

41 minutes ago
Our class watched the video. The students said they liked the pictures, the voices were not loud or clear enough, the speed of their talking was good, and overall they thought the video was ok

— Mrs. _____ class

Reply ·

42 minutes ago
Thank you for letting us watch your show. We liked it. We liked the little pig's house. We thought it was nice when the man shared his straw. We thought it was funny when he cooked the wolf and ate him.

We did not like the wolf when he blew down the house.

We think you are good readers.

— _____ Monkeys

Reply ·

18 hours ago
"I liked the story. It was good. The character Piglet was funny. The pictures were good because they were colorful. I liked the end when the wolf fell in the pot because he was bad " - _____

Reply ·

Teacher Reflection

Using technology to combine the written, audio, and visual components of storytelling into a digital composition and then uploading it to the web allowed students to share their work with their target audience — something that they couldn't have done without that technology. I saw tremendous effort and growth from some of my struggling writers in class. Some of the students who typically sit

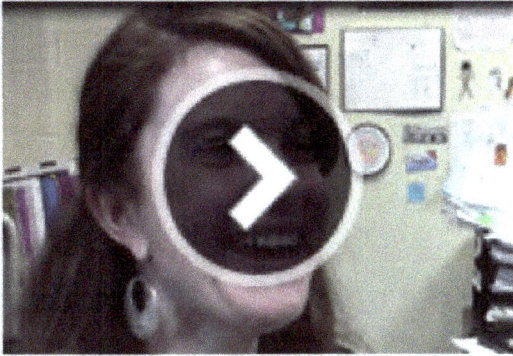

http://editlib.org/go/MS_ELA_Video10

for an hour with only a few sentences on their paper and hate writing, they were enthralled with this project. Those students benefited from the transition away from text and were finally given a way to share their voices with the world. Before I do this lesson again, I will explore more websites that students can use for both digital story creation and sharing their work with their audiences. Web 2.0 technologies emerge and change so much that by this time next year there may be something better available to me and to my students.

Classroom Management

The students worked very well together during this project. I tried to prevent classroom issues by giving very specific directions regarding student behaviors before breaking them into groups. My directions included simple things, like speak only to your group during class time, stay in your work station and don't disturb other groups, raise your hand when you have an issue rather than calling out and interrupting. We reviewed normal classroom procedures, like not leaving the room without permission and using reasonable volume levels while working together. Additionally, by creating the groups myself, I was able to separate some students who might have trouble remaining on task when working together.

Technology

For the most part, the technology worked really well. Whenever we use netbooks, there are always glitches that can come up in terms of the processor and recording audio, ensuring that it's a crisp, clean sound. Whenever that happens, we troubleshoot. Kids will say, "My netbook's not working right. Can I use your laptop?" But other than that, whenever there are problems, the kids are really able to help themselves and figure out what they need to do next. Part of that comes from being at a school with a 1-to-1 technology initiative where all students have a netbook.

I know a big fear for people whenever they use technology is that kids are going to use it in a malicious way. The most important thing you can do when you expose students to technology is to believe that they are going to do the right thing most of the time. Yes, they will find ways to do things that might not always be the best decision, but then it's important to have that open conversation just like you would if a kid was talking to another student across the classroom: Talk about why the behavior is not appropriate, and give the student a chance to learn from that mistake.

? How would you improve this activity or do it differently?

· · · · · · Resources ·

Common Core State Standards. (2014). Anchor standards: English language arts standards (College and Career Readiness Anchor Standards for Writing). Retrieved from http://www.corestandards.org/ELA-Literacy/CCRA/W/

National Council of Teachers of English. (2007a.) NCTE beliefs about the teaching of writing (NCTE Guideline). Retrieved from http://www.ncte.org/positions/statements/writingbeliefs

National Council of Teachers of English. (2007b.) Teaching composition: A position statement. (NCTE Guideline). Retrieved from http://www.ncte.org/positions/statements/teachingcomposition

High School English Language Arts

Jonathan Cohen | Marshall George | Dana Riddle

Interactive Activity

Before you begin the case study, please participate in the following interactive activity. This short learning experience will help you think about tone in poetry, the primary content focus of this case.

Watch and listen to the Lost Generation video at http://editlib.org/go/Sec_ELA_Video1. As you read the poem, listen carefully to the accompanying music. Does it capture the tone of the poem? If so, in what way? At what point does the music change?

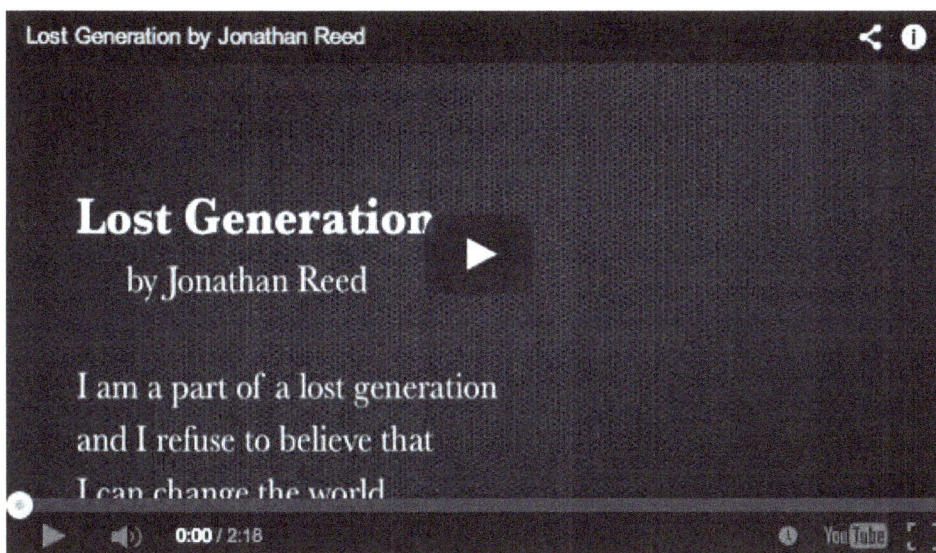

http://editlib.org/go/Sec_ELA_Video1

Now watch a second video at http://editlib.org/go/Sec_ELA/Video2. Pay attention to the voice of the narrator reading the poem, (which will scroll down the page). Does she capture the tone of the poem? At what point does her spoken tone change?

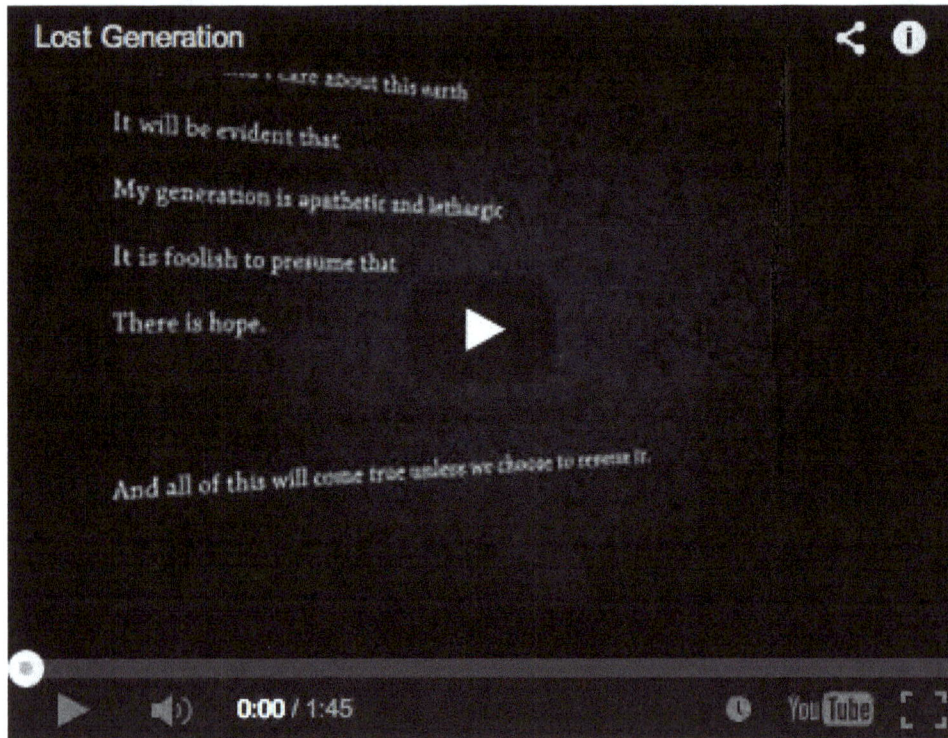

http://editlib.org/go/Sec_ELA_Video2

Did you notice the second half of the poem is the same as the first, only read in reverse? Take another look at the text. How might an English language arts (ELA) teacher use this poem to get students to think about tone in literature?

·Scenario

Interactions between and among human beings are complex and multidimensional. When one person engages in a conversation with another, each must read visual and verbal cues to make sense of what is being said. Understanding the tone of a speaker is crucial to understanding the speaker's meaning. Likewise, when reading literature, particularly poetry, understanding the tone of a text is critical to making meaning of it.

Because it is a somewhat abstract concept, tone, defined in literary study as the writer's or narrator's attitude toward the material and reader, is generally a difficult literary element to teach. While students are introduced to tone in elementary school, many middle and high school students still have difficulty identifying tone in a work of literature. Likewise, adolescents in English language arts classrooms sometimes struggle with making meaning from works of poetry.

The following activity presents a Digital Poetry Project from Dana Riddle's 10th-grade English language arts classrooms. With the use of web-based image libraries, Microsoft Movie Maker, a class wiki, and collaborative partnerships, students in the class explored tone in poetry while making connections between visual images and accompanying audio texts, thus enhancing their media and digital literacy.

Dana's activity is clearly aligned with standards, including those of the Common Core State Standards, the National Council of Teachers of English/International Reading Association standards, and the International Society for Technology in Education National Educational Technology Standards for Students.

Image via Flickr user thesaltr

Common Core State Standards

Following are examples of Common Core State Standards in English language arts grades 7-12 that are aligned with the activity that is presented in the video case. All standards related to Reading Literature include the study of poetry, among other genres.

- Determine the meaning of words and phrases as they are used in the text, including figurative and connotative meanings; analyze the cumulative impact of specific word choices on meaning and tone (e.g., how the language evokes a sense of time and place; how it sets a formal or informal tone).
- Gather relevant information from multiple print and digital sources, using search terms effectively.
- Use technology, including the Internet, to produce, publish, and update individual or shared writing products, taking advantage of technology's capacity to link to other information and to display information flexibly and dynamically.

National Council for Teachers of English/International Reading Association

- Students use a variety of technological and information resources (e.g., libraries, databases, computer networks, video) to gather and synthesize information and to create and communicate knowledge.
- Students adjust their use of spoken, written, and visual language (e.g., conventions, style, vocabulary) to communicate effectively with a variety of audiences and for different purposes.

International Society for Technology in Education NETS-S

- Locate, organize, analyze, evaluate, synthesize, and ethically use information from a variety of sources and media.
- Students demonstrate a sound understanding of technology concepts, systems, and operations.

What ideas do you have for helping students understand the concept of tone in literature?

Meet the Teacher · · · · · · · · · · · · · · · ·

- Dana Riddle
- English Teacher
- Albemarle High School

I am a certified teacher of English language arts in grades 6-12 and am beginning my third year of teaching. I have been at this school for all three years of my short career, and have taught grades 10 and 12 each year. I teach honors classes and academic advanced classes.

Despite my relatively short time in the classroom, I have been asked by the school's administration to lead professional development workshops for colleagues, mostly in the area of technology integration. I had good training in my teacher preparation program, and I see

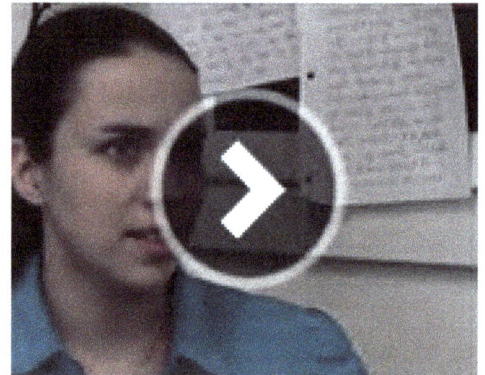

http://editlib.org/go/Sec_ELA_Video3

digital and media literacy as an integral part of the English
language arts curriculum.

http://editlib.org/go/Sec_ELA_Video4

As a teacher, I see myself as more of a mentor than an expert. I guess I am really a constructivist when it comes to teaching. My role is to come up with the best learning activities to help my students meet the objectives of the lesson or unit of study. Students learn best when they have ownership of what they are reading, writing, or creating, making personal connections to whatever we are doing in class.

Albemarle High School, where I teach, has been identified as rural and suburban. It is a high performing school with 96% of our students having proficiency in reading and 93% in math. Of our 1,750 students, about a third come from minority groups (17% Black; 6% Asian; 4% other groups). Close to 20% of our students come from economically disadvantaged homes. Despite the high level of achievement of the students in the class shown in the video case, I believe the activity is appropriate for students in other settings and contexts. I could see doing this lesson with students in grades 8-12.

The Activity

Toward the end of an instructional unit focusing on poetry Dana realized that some students were struggling to identify and articulate the tone of some of the more abstract poems they were reading. In an effort to help students better understand tone, she began a three-day lesson. Students spent most of each class period working on the assigned project in collaborative pairs. On the last day of the project, students turned from their role as producers to that of consumers. They watched the digital video projects created by their classmates and provided feedback and evaluation of their work.

Day 1

In the first part of the lesson sequence, Dana gave a mini-lesson reviewing the concept of tone in poetry. She and her students defined tone, created a list of terms that might be used to describe the tone of poems, and then read one poem together as a class and discussed the tone of the poem. Dana then instructed her students to revisit poems they had read during the poetry unit and identified the tones that could be found in the poems.

After having students watch and discuss the two "Lost Generation" videos you viewed at the beginning of this case, Dana explained the project that the students would be working on. In teams of two, students would select a poem that they liked and create a digital poetry project, in which they would combine visual images and digital recordings of them reading the poem to capture the tone and theme of the poem. They would have two class periods (in a block schedule) to create their projects and post them on their class wiki. On the third day, students would view projects of selected classmates and provide evaluative comments about their effectiveness.

TPACK Commentary: Students need opportunities to apply their understanding of abstract concepts such as tone. "I know it when I hear it," is a first step, but teaching for transfer requires that students engage in multiple interactions with the concept. Dana chose to use a mini-lesson to help students recall a prior discussion of tone. Then she had them apply the definition to familiar material, poems they have already read. Dana next showed two videos of a provocative poem. The multimodal presentation allowed students to experience the poem visually and aurally, further interacting with the concept, scaffolding their learning for the technology based digital poetry project.

Day 2

On Day 2, after a brief mini-lesson on oral interpretation of literature (how to use vocal features to represent tone and meaning when reading a work of literature) and a demonstration of Microsoft Movie Maker, students used the software to record two oral interpretive readings of their poems—one in a voice that expressed no tone and another that attempted to capture the tone of the poem. After the second recording, students listened to the audio recording, evaluated its effectiveness, and in most cases, re-recorded to better capture the tone of the poem. Most students made at least three recordings before being satisfied.

Once the digital audio recordings were complete, students paired them with the digital images to create a final product—a digital visual/oral poetry reading in Movie Maker. Dana felt that pairing visual images with the audio recordings would scaffold their understanding of tone, build their digital literacies (pairing video and audio files for effect), and motivate them to put greater effort into the project. Once they were satisfied with their work, they uploaded the projects to YouTube and then embedded the video project next to the text of their poem on the class wiki (which they had used throughout the year in their class).

Day 3

In the final stage of the lesson sequence, after a mini-lesson reviewing how to provide meaningful comments and critiques and reviewing the purpose of the digital video projects, student teams viewed classmates' digital poetry readings and responded to the presentations, using the wiki's comment feature to provide feedback. They were instructed to focus their evaluative comments on the poem's tone as captured in the digital images and oral interpretive reading. In the final part of the class period, student pairs were able to review their own digital poetry project a final time, read the comments and feedback of their classmates, discuss with their partners, and write a final reflection about what they had learned over the past three days—about tone, about media literacy, and about collaboration.

Dana assessed the students' project using a rubric that had elements related to content (understanding of theme and tone in poetry), use of images to capture theme and tone in a poem, use of oral interpretation and audio recording to do the same, and effectiveness in crafting a digital document that blended visual and audio files.

TPACK Commentary: An essential part of learning for transfer is knowing the extent and quality of what one learned. In this assignment, Dana asked students to compose for a public audience and then provide feedback on the presentations of classmates. Dana knew that using digital recordings of their oral interpretations of the poems provided a much better way for her students to demonstrate their understanding of tone than, say, a traditional formal literary analysis essay. The digital recordings could capture tone (which is really an oral tradition) more precisely than a written essay. Dana also realized that audio alone might not capture the tone and that, as they say, "a picture is worth a thousand words." Therefore, using Movie Maker to provide the added visual dimension both supported content and was more motivating for her students. Also, using videos and a wiki gave Dana's students a platform to take their work and their feedback public, which is both engaging and motivating. The written reflection offered a final way for individuals to articulate their learning, making it more likely that they will not only remember what tone is but also be able to comprehend and compose it in future texts.

? What are the benefits of having students work in pairs on this project rather than individually or in small groups?

The Technology

In this lesson Dana used several technologies, some of which her students were accustomed to using, others that were new to them. Students pasted the text of self-selected poems into the class wiki. They used Internet search engines to locate images that would convey their understanding of the tone and main ideas of their selected poems.

They used Windows Live Movie Maker, which was new to most of the students. Dana selected this program for three reasons: (a) it was already installed on the school-owned laptops that she uses with her students on a regular basis; (b) Movie Maker is fairly simple to use and interfaces smoothly with the laptops' built-in web camera and microphone; and (c) it is a relatively simple program that allows for all of the technical features this project required—audio and video clip joining and trimming, pairing of audio and visual, and easy uploading to YouTube. While some of Dana's students had previously uploaded to YouTube, many had not, so she had to support this portion of the process somewhat. Dana first did a quick demonstration for the entire class and then circulated to provide coaching as needed.

Dana and her class had utilized a wiki all year long in various ways. She posted assignments throughout the year, maintained a class assignment calendar, used a Twitter widget, and posted supplemental materials on the wiki.

http://bit.ly/ELAwiki

Likewise, the students used the wiki throughout the year to post response papers, journal entries, and book reviews. The students were comfortable with uploading their completed projects to the wiki and viewing each other's work. The comment feature in the wiki was essential to the feedback/response portion of the activity.

?

What technology support might students need to complete this activity?

How would you structure the activity so that you are available to support the technological questions and challenges your students might have with this activity?

What classroom management issues do you anticipate in your own classroom if you had your students engage in this activity?

What alternative technologies might you use if any of the ones that Dana used were not available to you and your students?

TPACK Commentary: Although much of the technology used in the digital poetry project was familiar to the students in Dana's class (with the exception of Movie Maker), she had never used them together in this way. She had several classroom management problems to solve due to the collaborative nature of the assignment (students working in pairs). She needed additional space for students to work, especially during the audio recording, so she had students use space in an empty adjacent classroom and had a colleague oversee them. She circulated constantly through her own classroom, as well as the one her students had annexed. As she moved about, she conferenced with students about their content understandings as well as their use of the technologies. Dana also identified technology "experts" in the class who could provide support to classmates while she was working with other students.

Classroom in Action · · · · · · · · · · · · · · · · · · ·

Students worked in pairs for two days to create this digital poetry project (the third day was for viewing and responding to each other's videos). Dana supported her students' learning of both the content and the technology. The collaborative project helped students better understand the concept of tone while simultaneously developing their digital and media literacies.

Vignette1

As Dana introduces this activity, watch for the strategies she uses to prepare students to use the technology as a tool for achieving her learning objective.

http://editlib.org/go/Sec_ELA_Video5

? Providing directions simultaneously on how to do the learning activity and how to operate a technology tool takes some forethought and pedagogical skill.

What did Dana do well in this introduction?

What could she have done more effectively to keep students engaged?

TPACK Commentary: Notice that Dana did not walk students through the Movie Maker software step by step. Rather, she focused on the particular features of the tools that they would be using to help demonstrate their understanding of tone in their work. She was very specific in what she wanted the students to do and how to integrate the use of the two different software applications, and she addressed this all in the context of the specific requirements and expectations of the project. In addition to these big-picture ideas, she also helped students avoid common challenges by having the students record their narration in the more quiet hallway and by providing tips on where to save and access the files. In short, the way Dana introduced the technology tools went beyond a techno-centric focus on the tools themselves to a more pedagogically focused introduction of the tools.

Vignette 2

In this portion of the lesson, one pair of students is working to create a digital audio recording of the text of the poem that captures the tones found in "Stopping by the Woods on a Snowy Evening" by Robert Frost. Dana monitored their progress with this part of the activity, providing feedback and support as needed. Note how she encourages the students to listen to their recordings critically to determine if they had adequately captured the tone in the poem.

http://editlib.org/go/Sec_ELA_Video6

? In what ways might requiring students to create digital audio recordings allow them to demonstrate their understanding of tone?

How might this be motivating for students who find the study of poetry to be challenging and uninteresting?

Vignette 3

After the projects were completed and uploaded to the class wiki, students spent time viewing the videos of their classmates. They were asked to discuss and evaluate the appropriateness of the tone portrayed in the oral interpretative recording. This part of the project is important, as there was a real audience for the project and the creators were able to get feedback and suggestions from that audience.

http://editlib.org/go/Sec_ELA_Video7

TPACK Commentary: Dana understood that basic technologies like a laptop with a microphone would afford the students the opportunity to explore oral interpretation and tone in a meaningful way. She provided technological support to the students by suggesting that they rename the file to a more easily memorable name and that they minimize the document as they review and reflect on their work. Clearly, Dana was familiar with the challenges students face when they need to curate multiple files and multiple drafts of digital files.

In the third vignette, Dana guided students to articulate their readers' response to oral poetry readings to provide feedback and reader response, using the comment feature on the wiki to which the recorded poetry readings had been recorded. Some of her comments focused on the content. For example, one student referred to the reader's tone as being lonely, and the other suggested that the selected image is dark. Dana pointed out that the creators of the project probably used the audio and visual effects to demonstrate a particular phrase in the text, "miles to go before I sleep." In that same interaction, she provided them with a suggestion for making the most of their collaborative time, having one person enter the comments on the wiki while the other call out the text.

Students' projects represented a range of poetry types, including lyrical, narrative, humorous, and whimsical. The two projects below focused on classic texts that high school students often read. Look at the two sample projects and think about what literacies the students who created them demonstrated in their work. Do they seem to understand tone? Her 10th graders' oral interpretation skills were rudimentary when they started the project, so Dana had to keep that in mind as she assessed their work.

http://editlib.org/go/Sec_ELA_Video8

http://editlib.org/go/Sec_ELA_Video9

Student comments on the wiki (which is private and cannot be shared here) focused on various aspects of the project. For example, one student posted, "The rise and fall of your voice as you read the second stanza made me feel like I was on the ship." Another student focused her comment on the pairing of digital images and the audio recording, saying, "Before you started reading, and I just saw the horse in the field [in the image], I wasn't sure what the tone was supposed to be, but when you started reading it I immediately knew that the tone was somber and contemplative." A review of the student comments showed that they focused almost equally on tone, visual imagery, oral interpretation in the audio recordings, and technological savvy.

Poetry is scary and confusing for a lot of kids, so I feel like this project, at this particular point in the poetry unit, was a really good idea. Some of my kids had been struggling with identifying tone. Some even struggled with it in this activity. I think that the process of having them complete this project coupled with the process of reviewing and critiquing the projects of their classmates helped the proverbial light bulb to go off for some of my kids. They really got a deeper understanding of the particular texts they were working with and felt some sort of ownership of the poems through the process of pairing the text of the poems with visual images and their audio recordings.

I feel like the use of technology in this lesson really led to students' better understanding tone. When they talk to one other in everyday conversation, they hear each other's tone but they don't have an awareness of their own tone of voice. This was true when they did their oral reading of the poems. When they had the opportunity to go back and listen to their recordings, they were able to self-assess the effectiveness of their attempt to capture the tone of the poem they were reading. If they were not satisfied with the tone they conveyed in the reading, they could go back and do another recording very quickly and easily. Some did it numerous times until they got the effect they wanted. We have talked a great deal in class about the writing process, and they are used to writing multiple drafts. I think the students realized (as did I) that creating audio recordings also requires revision and editing. This was an eye-opening experience for us all.

One of the logistical lessons I learned during this initial go round with this activity had to do with the process of saving a file in Movie Maker. Numerous students lost their work from day 2 of the activity, because they saved the movie as a project rather than as a movie (it seems logical that the unfinished piece would be a project, not a movie). Since the computers rebooted at the end of the day, those students who saved as projects lost their day's work. I learned my lesson about this. As this was my first time using Movie Maker in the classroom, I had no idea that I needed to provide this particular instruction to the students. Now I know. That is one of the challenges of working with new technology, but the students and I learned it rather quickly.

Another lesson learned had to do with the setup for recording the audio files. Because our classroom is relatively small, there was no quiet area for students to make their recording. I sent them into the hallway and an adjacent classroom to do it. For the most part this worked well, but for some students it was a struggle to stay focused outside my classroom. By identifying "recording specialists" who knew the ins and outs of audio recording, I was able to have help with trying to support each of the pairs of student in the class.

This was the first time I tried this project with my students. I definitely feel that it was worth the three days of instruction. Not only did my students come away with a better understanding of tone, they had a greater appreciation for the poetry that we had studied in class. They had made a personal connection to at least one of the poems. They also got to stretch their digital and media literacies by creating the digital poetry project. I like to experiment each year with something new. This one is a keeper.

? What other possibilities exist for a digital project like the one Dana and her students completed?

Could it be used for other literary genres?

TPACK Commentary: A close reading of Dana's comments show that she simultaneously thought about content, pedagogy, and technology as she reflected on the lesson plan, the pedagogical choices she made while facilitating the lesson, and the projects created by the students. When thinking about the technologies used in the project she linked them to the content objectives, the learning process, and the learning outcomes. She did not separate her discussions of the various aspects of the lesson; rather, she thought of them in a recursive, connected, and symbiotic way. She considered issues of classroom management related to the technologies being used and, quite adroitly, named "specialists" in audio recording, Movie Maker, and wiki management.

Resources

Common Core State Standards Initiative. (2014). *English language arts standards*. Retrieved from http://www.corestandards.org/ELA-Literacy/

National Council of Teachers of English and the International Reading Association. (2012). *NCTE/IRA Standards for the English language arts*. Retrieved from http://www.ncte.org/standards/ncte-ira

Elementary Math

William R. Kjellstrom | Robert Q. Berry | Paula White

· · · Interactive Activity ·

Before you begin the case study, please try the following interactive activity. This short learning experience will help you think about estimationas well as how to use a spreadsheet-based Estimation Calcuator.

Solve the following problem using an estimation strategy of your choosing. Enter the problem and your estimate in the spreadsheet-based Estimation Calculator (click on the image below and the spreadsheet will open in a new window or tab).

444 X 222 = ?

factors
444
X ▾ 222

solution, hidden. Make another estimate...

your estimate

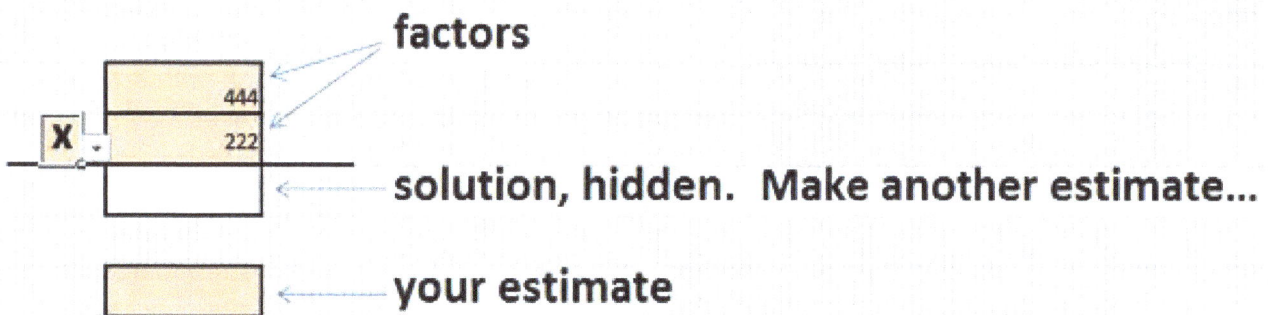

http://editlib.org/u/EL_M_Spreadsheet

Here is the Estimation Calculator's response to an estimate of 80,000:

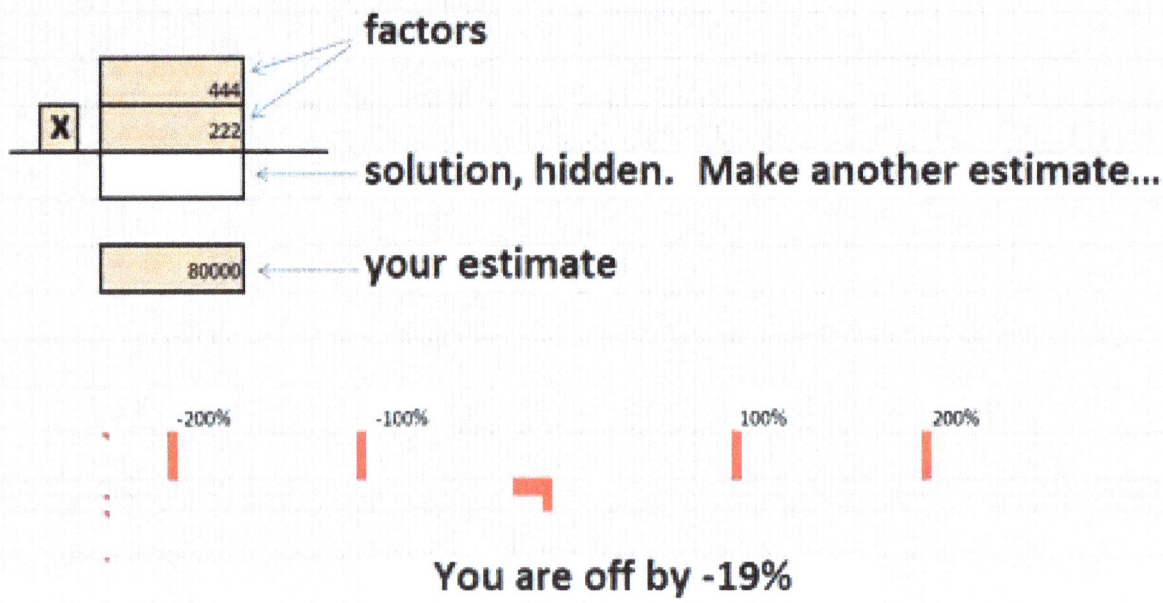

factors

444
222

solution, hidden. Make another estimate...

80000 → your estimate

-200%   -100%   100%   200%

You are off by -19%

- Did your estimate fall within the acceptable range?

- If not, how did you revise your estimate?

· · · · · · · Scenario ·

Have you ever estimated the total cost of a cart full of groceries as you entered the checkout line only to be shocked by the actual bill once the cashier rang up your purchases? Computational estimation is an important skill with applications in many areas of life outside the classroom. The consequences of underestimation at the grocery story are fairly benign, but when a medical technician is unable to recognize that health equipment is generating incorrect values, patients' lives may be at risk.

This chapter presents a rich media case study from Paula White's fifth-grade classroom that documents students' use of a web-based Flash application called the Estimation Calculator to enhance computational estimation. The Estimation Calculator was specifically designed to develop students' computational estimation strategies.

Computational estimation involves making reasonable approximations for arithmetic problems, and it differs from estimations of measurement and time. Computational estimation is a form of problem solving that calls on a variety of skills used daily by adults, yet many people have never received adequate instruction on effective estimation strategies.

Teachers can begin developing children's computational estimation abilities and expanding their range of estimation strategies in elementary school. Students are generally capable of the abstraction required for computational estimation by the late elementary grades, but explicit instruction and practice are essential.

Strong estimation abilities enhance children's number sense, place value recognition, and understanding of the relative magnitude of rational numbers. The Common Core State Standards for School Mathematics in both the Grade 3 and Grade 4 Operations and Algebraic Thinking standards suggest that students should be able to "assess the reasonableness of answers using mental computation and estimation strategies including rounding" (www.corestandards.org/math).

Additionally, the National Council for Teachers of Mathematics (NCTM) recommends that all elementary students learn how to effectively estimate both mentally and on paper:

> Develop and use strategies to estimate the results of whole-number computations and to judge the reasonableness of such results (Principals and Standards for School Mathematics, Number and Operations, Compute fluently and make reasonable estimates, Grade 3-5 Expectations)

Despite consensus among national organizations for flexible estimation approaches, students often learn only one strategy for estimating. A commonly employed strategy involves rounding to the largest place value without an understanding of how reasonable the estimate is in terms of the exact solution. For example, students in the upper elementary grades often learn to estimate by rounding to the largest place value (77 x 18 becomes 80 x 20) and solving the problem (1,600). Although the answer is technically correct and the estimation strategy is valid, students rarely consider how close the estimate is to the correct solution: 1,386. Rounding to the largest place value produces an estimate that is more than 15% higher than the actual answer.

Students need to understand that other strategies may bring them closer to the actual answer. Here are some other estimation processes students can use to generate a more reasonable estimate:

- **Translation**: Changing the operation or mathematical structure of a problem so that it is easier to estimate. For example, a translation strategy involves altering 18 + 22 + 24 to 20 x 3.

- **Reformulation**: Altering the numbers in a problem so that it is easier to find an estimate. For example, a reformulation strategy involves altering 18 + 22 + 24 to 20 + 20 + 20.

- **Compensation**: Adjusting an estimate based on changes made while translating or reformulating the original problem. For example, changing 29 x 24 to 30 x 20 (reformulation) produces an estimate of 600. Compensation occurs if the student then adds 120 to the estimate of 600 to counterbalance rounding 24 to 20.

In addition to being limited by their range of estimation strategies, students often possess one or more misconceptions about estimation as a result of years of focusing on algorithmic precision. For example, students often think that the exact answer is the only solution that is important. It follows, naturally, that estimation is a waste of time when emphasis is placed on exact calculations. Students must be convinced of the value of computational estimation before they will put effort into developing their skills. They must realize that computational estimation saves time and effort in the real world when there is not access to a calculator or when inputting information is too time consuming.

In many situations an estimate provides a useful check on a supposedly exact answer, even when using a calculator. Students should be reminded that a calculator yields a correct answer only if they enter the problem correctly. When students can appropriately estimate whether a calculator's answer is approximately correct, they can then go on to identify possible issues related to incorrectly entering the problem.

> **?**
>
> How might you help your students develop their computational estimation skills?
>
> How would you prompt elementary students to try alternative estimation strategies?
>
> What technology tools might you choose to help your students develop estimation skills?

Meet the Teacher

- Paula White
- Gifted Resource Teacher
- Crozet Elementary School

I am a certified gifted resource teacher at Crozet Elementary School in central Virginia and have taught kindergarten through fifth grade for thirty years, both as a regular classroom teacher and gifted resource specialist. I am a Google Certified Teacher, an Apple Distinguished Educator, and a STAR Discovery Educator.

My philosophy of teaching mathematics involves a mixture of direct instruction, discourse, and hands-on activities. I think that the teacher needs to provide enough instruction so that students have a direction but not so much that the teacher is dominating the learning experience. To this end, I place great value on asking questions that elicit students' thinking about content. Although not easy, questioning and listening are two keys to helping students move beyond a superficial understanding of mathematics. (Watch the video to learn more about Paula's teaching philosophy.)

http://editlib.org/u/EL_M_Video1

With regard to teaching estimation and estimation strategies, I believe that is important for students to be able to find a range of acceptable estimates that closely approximate the correct solution. Teaching a single approach to estimation, like rounding to the largest place value, insufficiently prepares students to judge the reasonableness of a slew of possible estimates! Students need a repertoire of strategies and time to practice them in order to be successful estimators.

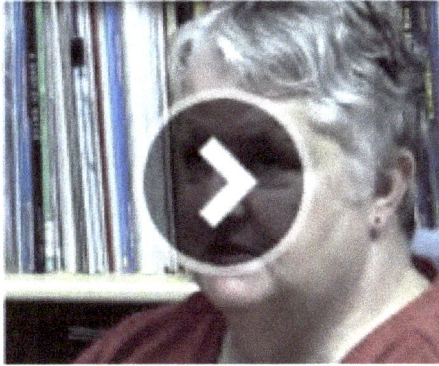

http://editlib.org/u/EL_M_Video2

The school where I teach is a small, rural school with approximately 300 students in kindergarten through fifth grade. Of these students, 24% receive free and reduced meals through federal assistance. Most of the students are White (86%); only 2.4% are African-American, 4.2% are Hispanic, and 3.5% are limited English proficient. The classroom in this case study had more females than males, which is not typical of the school in general. Of the 20 students in the class, all were classified as high performing in mathematics, with a smaller subset of the total group considered to be academically gifted. Despite the advanced characteristic of the class, I believe that this lesson is appropriate for all fifth-grade students.

· · · · The Activity · · · · · · · · · · · · · · · · · · ·

The activity described in this case study was the third in a series of learning experiences that focused on estimation and estimation strategies. The first two lessons focused on defining estimation, evaluating when to make an estimate and when to compute an exact answer, and reviewing the estimation strategies of translation, reformulation, and compensation. (Watch the video for more about Paula's rationale for focusing on the topic of estimation.)

My overarching objective for this lesson was to encourage students to use alternative estimation strategies based on the reasonableness of an initial estimate. I relied on the Estimation Calculator, a free web-based application, to guide students toward increased precision, and I explained to the students that verbalizing their mathematical thinking was extremely important. I also wanted students to have a contextual hook for why estimation was necessary, so I incorporated word problems that applied to the students' real lives. I made informal observations of students' conversations. At the end of the lesson, I assessed student learning formally through their written answers to questions.

http://editlib.org/u/EL_M_Video3

The lesson occurred in three parts: Introduction, Activity, and Conclusion.

Introduction

I reviewed what the students learned in the previous two lessons using a projected computer display and a document camera. We discussed what classified as estimation before beginning two sample word problems. Seated on a rug in front of a computer projector, students worked in pairs to solve the following problems as I circulated and assisted:

1. Crozet Elementary fifth-grade classes had a food drive for the Blue Ridge Area Food Bank. About how much was collected in all?

   Ms. W's class collected 346 pounds.
   Ms. X's class collected 402 pounds.
   Ms. Y's class collected 388 pounds.
   Ms. Z's class collected 327 pounds.

2. Eight people enter an elevator. The approximate weight of each person is 176 pounds. About how much weight is on the elevator?
   Is this over or under the maximum weight allowed (1,500 lbs)?

I went over the problems when the students finished, listened to the estimates they derived, and prompted them to explain their estimation strategies as they showed their work beneath the document camera. I then explained that they would be using the Estimation Calculator, a web-based application, to solve additional problems.

TPACK Commentary: Connecting previously learned content to the current lesson objectives creates a narrative arc that ties learning experiences together. Reviewing past lessons also enables the teacher to assess whether or not students grasp underlying concepts that are necessary for more complex tasks. In this case, Paula chose to use a projector and a document camera to review past work and the sample word problems. The document camera allowed students to share their work with the class in a convenient and easy way. Her decision to use these technologies related directly to their usefulness in accomplishing the learning objective.

Activity

The students began the activity by watching a screencast video about how to use the Estimation Calculator with a partner. The screencast was displayed on an iPod Touch®, and the students listened on shared earbuds as they worked through a sample problem. Once finished, students solved four problems designed to encourage use of multiple estimation strategies. The four problems were as follows.

1. 149 + 338

2. 449 + 144

3. 77 x 18

4. 26 x 59

For each problem, one partner was assigned the role of "worker," and this person made an estimate and verbalized the strategy that was used. The other student's role was to take notes and write down the worker's strategy. Once an estimate was made and the strategy was recorded, the worker entered the problem and the estimate into the Estimation Calculator. If the estimate was greater than 15% above or below the exact answer, the worker revised the estimate using a different estimation strategy. The students switched roles and moved to the next problem when a reasonable estimate was made.

?

What might be the benefits of having students watch a screencast on a small, portable media player while learning how to use a new technological tool?

What technology troubleshooting might be required when students use a tool like this?

How does Paula use student roles to maximize student participation in the activity?

Conclusion

The lesson's conclusion incorporated a synchronous, online discussion. I asked the students to enter responses to a question: "Is it better to overestimate or underestimate?" I then encouraged students to explain their reasoning with real-world examples.

The Technology

In this lesson Paula chose to use the Estimation Calculator, a software application developed specifically to develop students' skills in computational estimation, estimation strategies, and making reasonable estimates.

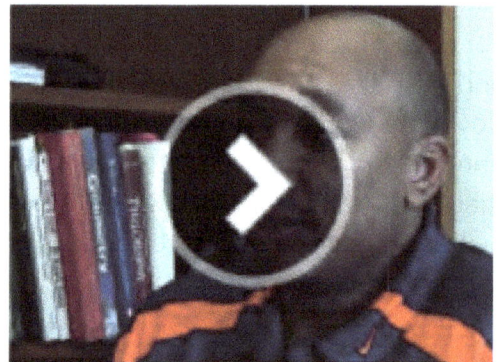

The Estimation Calculator provides a visual indicator of the reasonableness of an estimate within a certain percentage above or below the exact answer. Paula used this tool to encourage students to implement different estimation strategies for addition and multiplication problems

http://editlib.org/u/EL_M_Video4

involving whole numbers. The Estimation Calculator provides feedback on the reasonableness of estimates to mathematical problems. The Web-based application is no longer available, but you and your students can use a spreadsheet version that performs the same operations (http://editlib.org/u/EL_M_Spreadsheet. (Watch the video for further explanation of the Estimation Calculator by its creator, Robert Q. Berry III.)

Users enter an addition, subtraction, multiplication, or division problem as well as an estimated solution, and the Estimation Calculator displays a graphic and numeric indicator that shows how close the estimate is to the correct answer. If the estimate is within +/- 15% of the answer, then the Estimation Calculator will display the correct solution. Users are prompted to try again if the estimate is outside of the range. Visual feedback is an important component within the Estimation Calculator.

Using the Estimation Calculator to provide feedback for making reasonable estimates aligns with the following ISTE National Educational Technology Standards for Students (NETS-S):

- **Research and Information Fluency**: Students apply digital tools to gather, evaluate, and use information.

- **Critical Thinking, Problem Solving, and Decision Making**: Students collect and analyze data to identify solutions and/or make informed decisions.

If you could create the ideal tool for helping students develop their computational estimation skills, what features would it have?

What technological preparation would students need before using the Estimation Calculator most effectively?

What classroom management strategies would you use to keep students on task with this assignment?

How might you use this technology with a class of students who are not high performing in mathematics?

Classroom in Action

Throughout the activity portion of the lesson, receiving feedback on the reasonableness of an estimate became an impetus for students' use of various estimation strategies.

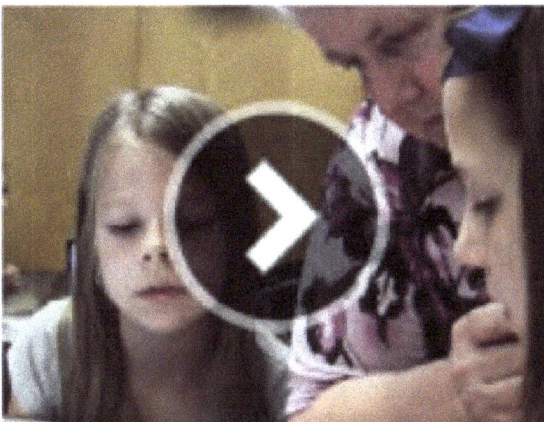

http://editlib.org/u/EL_M_Video5

What estimation processes did the student used to arrive at the initial and final estimate? (reformulation, translation, and/or compensation)

What kinds of open-ended questions did Paula ask to encourage the student to reconsider her estimate?

Watch the following video clip and pay attention to how Paula elicited the student's estimation strategy. Think about what might have happened if Paula did not ask the student to explain her estimation process.

http://editlib.org/u/EL_M_Video6

? What estimation processes did the student use to solve the problem?

How did Paula incorporate mathematical language like "compatible numbers?"

In these vignettes, what evidence did you observe that students were learning and developing their estimation skills?

TPACK Commentary: Students often search for the correct solution when working math problems. Arriving at the answer is sometimes seen as the goal, and the mathematical thinking that underlies the solution goes unnoticed without teacher guidance and prompting. However, when a skilled educator prods and prompts students to explain their thinking, insights into both students' conceptual understanding and their misconceptions are revealed. In the first vignette, Paula used the visual feedback bar in the Estimation Calculator to prompt the girl to revise her strategy. The questions that she asked are broad but guiding in that they facilitate more precise rounding. In the second vignette, Paula simply asked the student to explain her thinking so that she knows the estimation strategy that was used.

Assessing Written Documentation

Students were scattered throughout the room during the activity portion of the lesson. Some were sitting on the floor beneath the whiteboard, others at desks, and a few lounging on the classroom couch. As I walked around and observed, I saw that most students were busily discussing their estimation strategies with their partner. I immediately noticed that students were having rich discussions about the problems. They were checking their estimates on the estimation calculator and, in many cases, revising their strategies. However, the conversations clearly did not correlate with what was being written on their worksheets.

For example, one pair had a rich dialog about how to estimate 26 x 59. The student making the estimate for this problem explained that rounding to the tens place for both numbers (30 x 60) produced an estimate of 1,800, which was outside of the range of a reasonable approximation based on the Estimation Calculator. The student then rounded 26 to 25 and explained that rounding down would produce a more accurate estimate because the rounded number was closer to the original number. When I looked at the written account of this pair's estimation strategies, I immediately saw that the original attempt to estimate was not documented nor was the explanation about why 25 was a better approximation of 26. Had I not witnessed the conversation, I would have never known that these students were wrestling with alternative strategies.

4. The Worker's Problem 4: 26 x 59

The Worker's Estimate for Problem 4: _____ 1500

The Note Taker's Description of the Estimation Strategy:

_____

_____

_____

Why did the estimation strategy work or not work? Why?

_____

_____

_____

I reviewed all of the worksheets and saw a lack of written clarity and specificity much like the previous example. It was almost as if the conversations were too complex and too long for the students to clearly capture in the space provided. Yet, I wanted the students working in pairs and talking to each other, because I believed that verbally sharing encouraged students to expand their repertoire of strategies and approaches. In my opinion, mathematical discourse was a powerful way to strengthen conceptual knowledge of estimation.

I would consider audio recording the conversations in the future instead of having them write the dialog on a worksheet. For me, understanding thought processes is more important then having a tangible, written artifact. I also think that audio recording would provide the class with opportunities to hear other individual's estimation strategies. Yet, recording potentially creates more overhead in terms of saving files and instructing students on how to use an audio recorder.

? How would you address the issue of students insufficiently describing their thought processes on paper?

How would you assess students' learning growth after this activity?

Cumulative Assessment

I gave all of the students a short written assessment on the day after the lesson. The assessment included questions for the upcoming unit as well as two questions pertaining to estimation. The first estimation question was a 4-digit by 4-digit subtraction problem, and the second question was a 2-digit by 2-digit multiplication problem. I asked the students to estimate the answer and describe the estimation strategy that they used to arrive at the approximation. Students wrote their answers on paper and did not use the Estimation Calculator to check for reasonableness. I chose not to use the Estimation Calculator in the assessment because I wanted to see whether or not students would use alternative strategies that did not involve rounding to the largest place value without being prompted by the tool's visual feedback.

The results were quite interesting! All of the students used a variety of strategies to solve both of the problems even when not using the Estimation Calculator. The subtraction problem produced the most diverse set of answers (9,644 - 5,788). One student articulated that he initially rounded both numbers to the hundreds place (9,600 - 5,800). He then realized that the rounded numbers were not easy to mentally subtract, so he rounded 9,644 to 10,000 and then subtracted 5,800 from 10,000 to arrive at his estimate (4,200).

Although rounding to the largest place value would have resulted in a reasonable estimate on the Estimation Calculator had it been used, this student chose to use a more precise estimation strategy that involved compatible numbers. I am fairly certain that this student would not have answered the question in the same way had he not practiced problems using the Estimation Calculator.

Students also wrote clearer descriptions of their strategies on the assessment than what was shown on the worksheets during the lesson. There was much more detail, and I could clearly follow the strategy that was used to arrive at the estimate. I am unsure if the results are a reflection of the fact that the questions appeared in an assessment or if it was because they were working individually. Regardless, I was pleased to see that the students were able to articulate an estimation strategy clearly.

? How would you improve this activity?

In what ways could the learning goals be approached in a different way?

Teacher Reflection

Incorporating the Estimation Calculator into my estimation lessons forced students to think about using different strategies. Students were less reliant on basic rounding and more adept at examining the original numbers as clues for creating an estimate after the lesson. I believe that this change was a result of the visual feedback that the Estimation Calculator provided. Even though some were quite good at finding an arithmetically correct estimate, seeing how far away the estimate was from the exact answer made students reconsider both their answer as well as the process for achieving the solution. Students internalized the need to make more precise estimates, and many demonstrated this understanding on problems that did not include the Estimation Calculator.

Two key components in this lesson's success were paired collaboration and probing questions. Students listened to their partner's estimation strategies and, in many instances, offered their personal approach without being prompted. This was especially true when the Estimation Calculator showed that an estimate was unreasonable and outside of the 15% range. The exchange of ideas in a one-on-one, student-to-student situation enhanced the applicability of various strategies in ways that a more teacher-centered, directive manner would fail to achieve. Yet, I was able to intercede and ask open-ended questions when conversations either stalled or lacked a full explanation. I even overheard students asking for clarification. Asking questions was very important because I wanted to understand how each child was thinking mathematically.

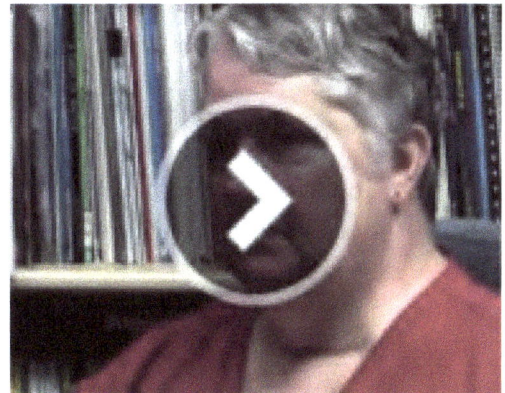

http://editlib.org/u/EL_M_Video7

http://editlib.org/u/EL_M_Video8

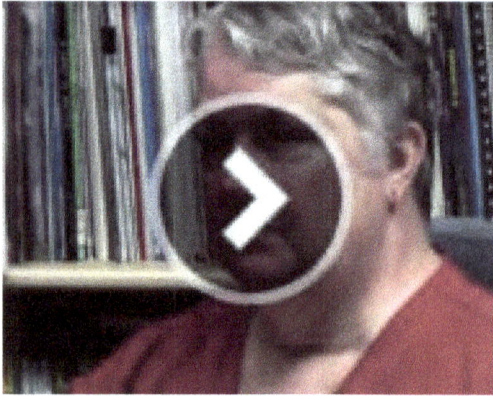

I did not experience any major classroom management issues with the technology. I am certain that this was a result of the cumulative experiences that the students have using various tools on a daily basis. The students knew my expectations of their technology use, and they acted accordingly. However, that does not mean that everything went smoothly! One problem that became quite apparent was that the sound quality on the iPod units was very poor when played through the built-in speakers. Students could not hear what was being said in the video when they were learning how to use the Estimation Calculator. Luckily, the students adapted by grabbing a pair of headphones and sharing the earbuds. When I teach the lesson again, I will make sure to include headphones or show the video on individual computers.

? Consider your classroom. What potential classroom management issues exist that might prevent you from successfully incorporating a tool like the Estimation Calculator?

Resources

Common Core State Standards Initiative. (2014). High school: Geometry– Modeling with geometry. Retrieved from http://www.corestandards.org/Math/Content/HSG/MG/

International Society for Technology in Education. (2014) ISTE Standards. Retrieved from http://www.iste.org/STANDARDS

High School Geometry

Nancee Garcia | Marilyn Strutchens

Interactive Activity

Before beginning this case study, try out this introduction to Geogebra. It is a free dynamic geometry tool available for the mathematics classroom that will allow you to explore characteristics of the centroid of a triangle (available at www.geogebra.org). Other similar tools like Geometer's Sketchpad are available, but are not free to use.

Go to Construct the Centroid (http://www.geogebratube.org/student/m12853) and use the strategy of your choosing to construct the centroid of a triangle, that is, the point where the three medians of a triangle intersect. For assistance, you can view the tutorial on how to use GeoGebra (http://wiki.geogebra.org/en/Main_Page).

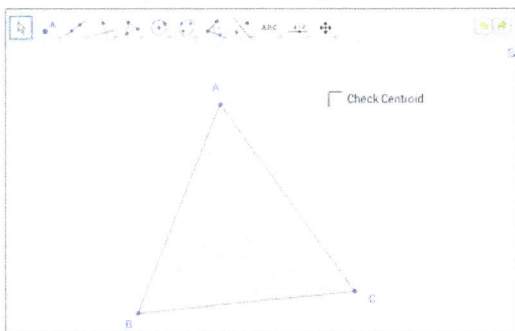

- Did you construct the centroid correctly before clicking on 'Check Centroid'?
- If not, how did you determine the error(s) in your sketch?
- What happens to the centroid as you click on and drag point A to different locations?
- Does the centroid ever lie outside the triangle? Why or why not?

The primary technology tool used in the case that follows is Geometer's Sketchpad, another dynamic geometry software tool that is sold commercially. As you explore each of these two programs, consider their different affordances and constraints.

Scenario

Students are commonly assigned problems in a high school geometry class that are unconnected to a real-world application and that do not require critical decision-making skills to solve. However, knowledge of geometry is essential to many design and construction careers such as engineering, plumbing, architecture, and graphic design and is used to make vital decisions to ensure public safety and minimize costs. Students need opportunities to experience how geometry can be used to make informed decisions about the world around them.

High school geometry students may explore various lines or segments in a triangle that are concurrent, such as angle bisectors or medians. The different points of concurrency studied in a high school geometry course are referred to as centers of a triangle. The properties of centers of a triangle make them useful locations in many design and construction problems, but they are not commonly explored in this way.

This rich media case features students in Nancee Garcia's high school geometry course exploring centers of triangles using Geometer's Sketchpad software to solve a real-world geometric design problem.

Students sometimes incorrectly assume that all triangles have a single center point as seen in other shapes, such as regular polygons and circles. However, several different triangular centers can be located, including the incenter, centroid, orthocenter, and circumcenter.

When the various centers of triangles formed by the concurrent (intersecting) lines, such as angle bisectors, perpendicular bisectors, medians, and altitudes, are constructed using traditional

Centers of triangles constructed using Geometer's Sketchpad©

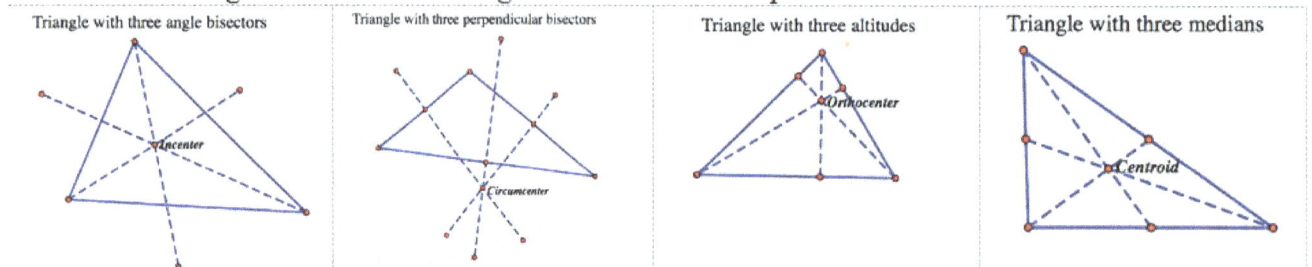

Triangle with three angle bisectors | Triangle with three perpendicular bisectors | Triangle with three altitudes | Triangle with three medians

construction tools like a straight edge and compass, many difficulties and misconceptions can arise for students.

For example, due to minor construction errors three medians may be constructed so that they appear not to be concurrent. Students may draw incorrect conclusions based on those errors. If medians are not drawn to the center of each vertex and midpoint, the medians do not appear to be intersecting at the same point. However, medians of a triangle are always concurrent.

Also, the multiple constructions and precise measurements required for this type of investigation can become tedious and lead to low levels of motivation when students must complete them by hand. Although geometric construction and precise measuring skills by hand are certainly important to develop in students, these skills are neither the purpose nor learning objective of this particular investigation and may cause frustration or incorrect conclusions or may impede the intended goals of the lesson.

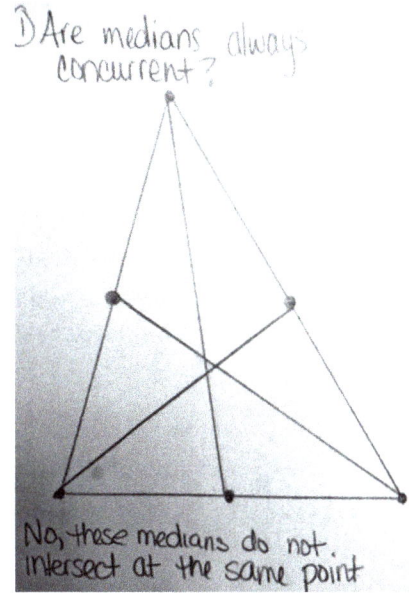

Hand-drawn errors leading to incorrect conclusions.

Solving a design problem such as this requires students to reason about the geometry and to make sense of the geometry in the context of the problem. Reasoning and sense making as described in the National Council of Teachers of Mathematics' Focus in High School Mathematics: Reasoning and Sense Making in Geometry (King, Orihuela, & Robinson, 2010) requires developing reasoning habits by students. Reasoning and sense-making are described as the purpose and means for mathematics learning, without which students view mathematics as an unrelated and complex set of rules to be memorized.

The Common Core State Standards include content objectives that emphasize the application of mathematical knowledge and also require engagement in Mathematical Practices. In particular, students are challenged to "apply geometric methods to solve design problems (e.g., designing an object or structure to satisfy physical constraints or minimize cost, working with typographic grid systems based on ratios)." (Common Core: Applying Geometric Knowledge)

Students cannot use mathematics effectively only by knowing mathematical facts and rules. They must also be able to apply the concepts. However, high school geometry students often have few opportunities to apply their mathematical knowledge to meaningful and significant problems. Problems that involve applying multiple mathematical concepts such as geometric design problems that minimize cost, time, and so forth, are even less frequently seen in the high school classroom. An advantage to using a dynamic geometry tool is that solving complex problems may be less time-consuming and more accessible to all students.

Common Core: Standards for Mathematical Practice

The lesson featured in this case was designed to engage students in several of the mathematical practices.

1. Make sense of problems and persevere in solving them.
2. Construct viable arguments and critique the reasoning of others.
3. Model with mathematics.
4. Use appropriate tools strategically.
5. Attend to precision.

> **?** How might you help students develop their skills to apply geometric concepts to the real world?
>
> What difficulties might students face when engaging in activities that require geometric design skills?

· · · · · · · Meet the Teacher · · · · · · · · · · · · ·

- Nancee Garcia
- Geometry and Discrete Mathematics Teacher
- Auburn High School

I am a high school geometry and mathematics teacher in Auburn, Alabama. I have taught geometry for 10 years, and I have also taught algebra, algebra II, IB math higher level and discrete mathematics. I am currently also a doctoral student at Auburn University pursuing my Ph.D. in mathematics education, with a special interest in using technology in the mathematics classroom.

Auburn High School is a diverse school in the state of Alabama due to its proximity to Auburn University and large multinational corporations. Of its 1,600 students, 27% are African-American, 8% are Asian, and 2% are Hispanic. In addition, there are 42 different languages spoken among the student population. On average, 20% of my students are classified as special education and require special services.

http://editlib.org/u/S_M_Video1

http://editlib.org/u/S_M_Video2

My overarching philosophy of teaching is that all students must be given the opportunity to learn mathematics, and it is the responsibility of the teacher to adapt to the learning needs of students. My goal for students when they leave my class is not to be able to recite a dozen formulas from memory but rather to have gained an appreciation for mathematics. I want them to see the usefulness of mathematics, that it is used to explain the world around them and to help them make important decisions. However, the bottom line is I must provide the opportunities for my students to see mathematics as useful in their lives.

I believe that the most important skills students can gain in my class are critical thinking and problem solving skills. My decision to use technology frequently in my classroom is in part based on my belief that students need to be comfortable using different types of technology for problem solving and investigating ideas. Particularly in geometry, Geometer's Sketchpad helps students to create examples and test their ideas such as exploring a shape to identify its properties or whether the properties will change when the shape is manipulated.

The Activity

The lesson highlighted in this case, Building a Shopping Center, is the third in the lesson sequence. The goal of the first lesson in the unit was for students to construct a centroid by finding the point of concurrency for the three medians of a triangle.

Students discovered that medians are always concurrent. They also identified the center of gravity or balancing point of various triangles as the centroid and the properties related to measurements of segments formed by the construction. The objective of the second lesson was to determine if the angle bisectors, perpendicular bisectors, and altitudes of a triangle are also concurrent. While the first lesson was completed using traditional construction tools, the second was completed using Geometer's Sketchpad.

In the third lesson, Building a Shopping Center, students worked in pairs and acted as members of a town planning committee to decide on the best place to build a shopping center that would serve three surrounding towns. I explained to students that their arguments must be supported by mathematical findings and account for the various constraints of the problem. Students were to use Geometer's Sketchpad (GSP) to explore and test their ideas and also to create a model of the situation to support their argument.

I informally assessed their understanding throughout by questioning their findings and listening to the dialogue between pairs. At the end of the lesson, students were formally assessed as they presented their final arguments.

Two class periods were required for this lesson. During the first day, I introduced the activity to students and most of the investigation was completed. The second day began with a summary of some findings from the first day, and then the pairs finished their investigations and prepared their arguments. The class ended with the presentations by the pairs.

To begin, I projected the instructions on an electronic whiteboard and discussed the scope of the activity with the class. Students also had summary notes from the previous day's lesson to serve as reminders of how each center was constructed.

Building a Shopping Center

A committee has been formed to help three towns decide where to build a new shopping center somewhere in the triangular area below designed to serve all three towns equally.

However, the committee cannot agree on where to build the shopping center. Their arguments are presented below.

Committee member A: Since each town is responsible for building the road to their own town, we need to put the shopping center at a location so that no town will have to build a longer (thus more expensive) road than the other two.

Committee member B: Instead of building roads to each town, it would be more economical to each build a road from the shopping center to one of the streets already going into our towns. Of course, no town should have to build a longer road than any of the other two towns.

Committee member C: We should build the shopping center at the place where the sum of the lengths of the roads directly to our towns is the least and then we can just split the cost three ways.

Students ended the activity by presenting to the class their decision about which was the best argument and why. Students displayed their work in GSP on the SMARTBoard as they presented. I assessed students' presentations and also assessed their understandings further by asking unexplored questions during their presentations.

TPACK Commentary: The objectives of the lesson provided a perfect opportunity for the use of technology, in particular the use of a dynamic software program, such as Geometer's Sketchpad (GSP). The use of GSP enabled the students to make conjectures and test them out, and it allowed the students to have more precision than they would have had if they only used paper and pencil. The use of GSP and the multiple entry-level task enabled Nancee to create a lesson that was inquiry based and motivating for the students. She could utilize the software in a number of ways to help the students understand the problem and to help them make sense of their own responses. The task and GSP together enable Nancee to ask rich thoughtful questions that pushed students to think more deeply about the content of the problem and whether or not their solutions made sense.

? What are the benefits of having students work in pairs on a technology–enriched project such as this one rather than individually or in small groups?

The Technology

Geometer's Sketchpad (GSP) is an effective tool for encouraging conjecturing, exploring, and reasoning by students. It includes tools to construct, draw, measure, and manipulate geometric objects such as points, lines, rays, and circles. It also allows students to do the following:

• Control and reason about the behavior of geometric objects
• Utilize the constraints or properties of objects to make constructions
• Find patterns and properties and test them to determine their generalizability
• Test and refine conjectures.

GSP has many advantages over more traditional methods of exploring geometric objects, such as performing manipulations not possible with ruler and compass (that is, objects retain properties related to the construction when manipulated) and making efficient and precise revisions and measures.

For this activity in particular, GSP allows students to construct each triangle center and find the measurement properties associated with it efficiently and accurately in order to investigate the best possible option for building the shopping center. Without the technology, students would likely get frustrated with the large amount of constructions required to fully investigate each possibility and most likely would not explore different types of triangles.

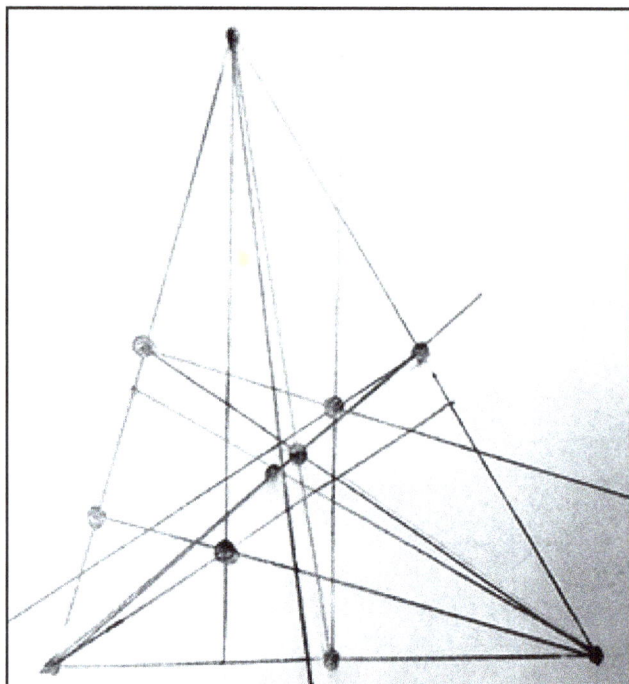

Hand-drawn construction showing four centers of a triangle and the lines used to create the centers.

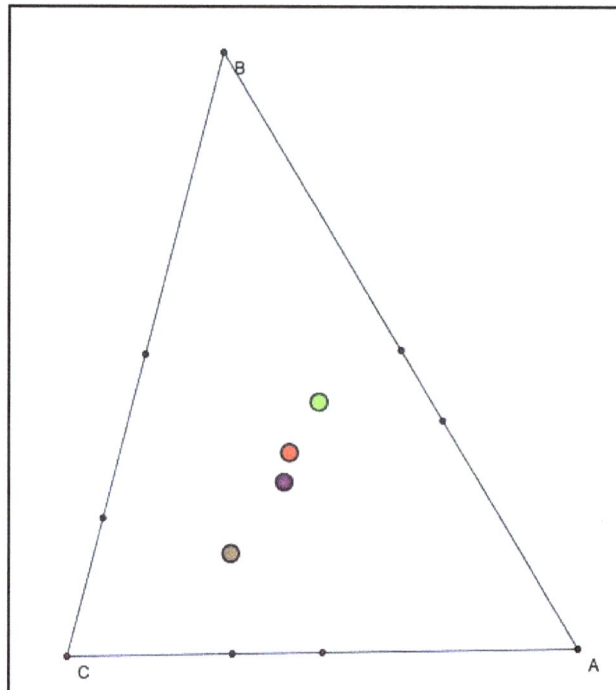

Geometer's Sketchpad construction showing four centers of a triangle with the lines creating the centers hidden.

Finally, students would find it difficult and confusing to construct all four centers on a triangle with pencil and paper in order to find the center that has the smallest sum when measuring each road from the center to each of the towns. With GSP students can construct each of the centers and then hide the various lines used to make the construction. They can then observe how the centers behave without the chaos of the 12 different lines needed to construct them.

This lesson addresses the following standards established by the International Society for Technology in Education (ISTE):

ISTE Standards for Teachers

Facilitate and Inspire Student Learning and Creativity – Engage students in exploring real-world issues and solving authentic problems using digital tools and resources.

Critical Thinking, Problem Solving, and Decision Making: Students use critical thinking skills to plan and conduct research, manage projects, solve problems, and make informed decisions using appropriate digital tools and resources. Students:

http://editlib.org/u/S_M_Video3

a. Identify and define authentic problems and significant questions for investigation.
b. Plan and manage activities to develop a solution or complete a project
c. Collect and analyze data to identify solutions and/or make informed decisions
d. Use multiple processes and diverse perspectives to explore alternative solutions (Standard 4)

? What knowledge of students, pedagogy, technology, and content did Nancee display in preparing, planning, and teaching this lesson?

· · · · Classroom in Action ·

During the activity each pair of students had a sheet on which to record their ideas as they explored. They were encouraged to construct each of the centers of the triangle they were familiar with and use measurements to determine if any of the centers could be used as the shopping center location described in the arguments from three committee members.

For example, students measured the distance from a center to each of the sides of the triangle in order to determine if the distances were equal as described by committee member B's argument. Several students had difficulty measuring the distance from a point to a line using a perpendicular segment.

Vignette 1: A window into student thinking

As you watch this next video, think about how Nancee recognizes the student's mistake then helps the student to see her misconception and fix her errors.

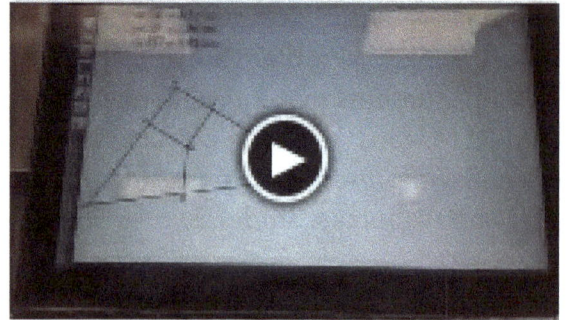

http://editlib.org/u/S_M_Video4

?

What might Nancee have observed that caused her to question the student's answers?

What misconception did the student hold about the distance from a point to line? How did Nancee's questioning and the technology help the student to recognize her misconception?

In what other ways could Nancee have helped the student to understand and correct her misconception through the use of technology?

TPACK Commentary: In this vignette Nancee knew that the distances should be equal. The technology allowed her to see that the distances were measured incorrectly and to diagnose the misconception by examining the student's sketch. Nancee observed that the center appeared to be an incenter, so she quickly scanned the picture to determine if the segments from the center to the sides of the triangle were perpendicular. After realizing that they were not, she encouraged the student to consider how she might have measured incorrectly. One commonly noted advantage to using dynamic geometry software is that teachers are able to see evidence of student thinking and understanding. For example, the choices of action that a student takes in a dynamic geometry environment often reflect the conceptions a student holds about the mathematics and the behavior of geometric objects in a constrained environment. Another important component of TPACK is that teachers have knowledge of which concepts are difficult to learn and ways that technology can help students to overcome the difficulties. In this case, the concept of the distance from a point to a line caused many misconceptions.

Vignette 2:

One of the triangle centers, the orthocenter, can lie inside, outside, or on the triangle when the triangle is acute, obtuse, or right, respectively. Students had to consider two different constraints when deciding whether or not the orthocenter was a possible location for the shopping center. The problem does not require a certain type of triangle but does require that the shopping center be located inside the triangle.

Watch the following video clip and pay attention to the ways that students communicate about and manage the various constraints in the problem that must be considered when finding a solution.

http://editlib.org/u/EL_M_Video6

? In what ways did the technology aid the students in making conclusions about the orthocenter?

In this interaction, what did you notice about the questions that Nancee asked the students? What did the questions require the students to do?

TPACK Commentary: Efficiency of computations and constructions is an important advantage when using technology to solve complex problems in mathematics. The ease with which the students were able to manipulate the triangle added complexity to the problem, since they were more likely to consider all types of triangles rather than just one acute, obtuse, or right triangle. Reasoning and making conclusions about "all possible" triangles (the general case) rather than one specific example (the particular case) is an important skill needed for constructing formal proofs. Students must have opportunities to move from reasoning about the particular case to the general case in order to develop the skills needed to engage in high-level proof and reasoning. This type of activity that acts as a bridge between informal and formal proof is all too often left out of geometry courses that include rigorous proof.

Vignette 3: Thinking through results

When exploring the measures of the distances from the circumcenter to each town, the students in the next video questioned the reasonableness of their findings when the results did not match their predictions. Nancee encouraged students to think critically by encouraging them to reason about solutions given by the technology tool instead of simply accepting any result as true.

The students in the video are suppose to measure the distances from the circumcenter to each of the vertices of the triangle. Instead, a student inadvertently measured the distance from a vertex to the midpoint of a side that was located extremely close to the circumcenter.

In the next video clip watch how Nancee guided the student, and listen to the student's observations and reflections.

http://editlib.org/u/S_M_Video6

? What specific pedagogical actions does Nancee take as a result of her technological, pedagogical, and mathematical knowledge?

How might you help students establish a routine of checking the reasonableness of technology-produced results?

TPACK Commentary: A common barrier to technology use in the mathematics classroom is the misconception that technology replaces student learning and understanding. In fact, the use of technology should enhance student learning and understanding. However, teachers must be aware of the ways that students can misuse technology and guide students to become more effective users. In this vignette, it is clear that Nancee has encouraged her students to verify and critique the results given by technology.

Vignette 4: Exploring even more

The point can be found where the sum of the distances to the vertices of the triangle is the least, but it was not one of the four centers that students were exploring. This figure shows that point, known as the Fermat point.

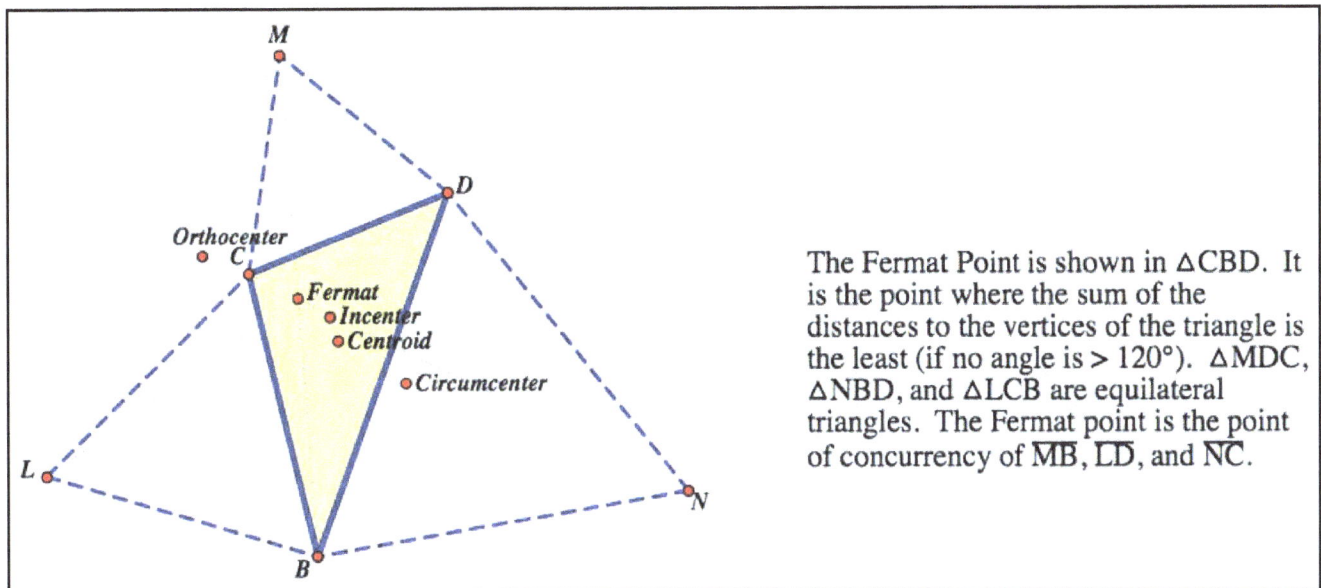

The Fermat Point is shown in △CBD. It is the point where the sum of the distances to the vertices of the triangle is the least (if no angle is > 120°). △MDC, △NBD, and △LCB are equilateral triangles. The Fermat point is the point of concurrency of $\overline{MB}$, $\overline{LD}$, and $\overline{NC}$.

Some students, due to the relative ease of creating multiple sketches and testing conjectures, explored other points to find a better solution. These students went above and beyond the requirements of the exploration, as their own curiosity challenged them to think about other possible solutions.

Watch the next video and notice how Nancee prompts the students to think about the feasibility of recommending a point that seems to be located in a random manner.

http://editlib.org/u/S_M_Video7

? Why do you think Nancee encouraged the students to reconsider using their random point? How would you have responded to a student that seemed to have found a better solution?

How could Nancee have helped her students to discover the Fermat point?

Student Work

Students realized throughout day that one "best" solution was not well defined. The committee members' arguments focused on the roads that needed to be built, so the class decided through discussions that the best solution would mean that the cost of the roads that the towns had to build should be minimized. Students summarized their work on their papers and on their GSP sketch they prepared for their presentations. The following is an example of each.

Reminder of the centers of triangles

Segments of Triangle	Sketch	Point of Concurrency	Properties
Altitudes		orthocenter-intersection of 2 or more lines	orthocenter is inside when it is an acute angle, outside when it is an obtuse angle, and on the triangle when it is a right angle.
Angle Bisectors		incenter	Point of concurrency always stays inside the triangle.
Perpendicular Bisectors		circumcenter	same properties as altitude
Medians		centroid	doesn't leave the center of the triangle.

Student Reference Chart

Argument	Location of shopping center and strategy used to find it	Notes and properties related to the location
A: put the shopping center at a location so that no town will have to build a longer road than the other two	Here you would use the circumcenter to base the road construction off of	Only works some of the time. It ends up being outside of the triangle when in an obtuse triangle so as we know you can't do that
B: each build the same length road from the shopping center to one of the streets already going into our towns	You do the angle bisector of each angle, then use the roads going from each already made road to that point, you use those three segments which are the same distance from each road, and that's where the mall goes	You make the roads from the incenter to each side of the triangle which all end up being the same distance apart
C: the place where the sum of the lengths of the roads directly to our towns is the least	For this you would find the altitudes and then use the orthocenter to base your roads off of	This works with acute triangles but with an obtuse triangle the orthocenter is found outside of the triangle. So this would work with some of the triangles but not all, so not the most reliable of all the options

Your Decision: I think council member B's idea is the best idea because it is the most reliable and the most cost efficient option.

Exploration Recording Sheet

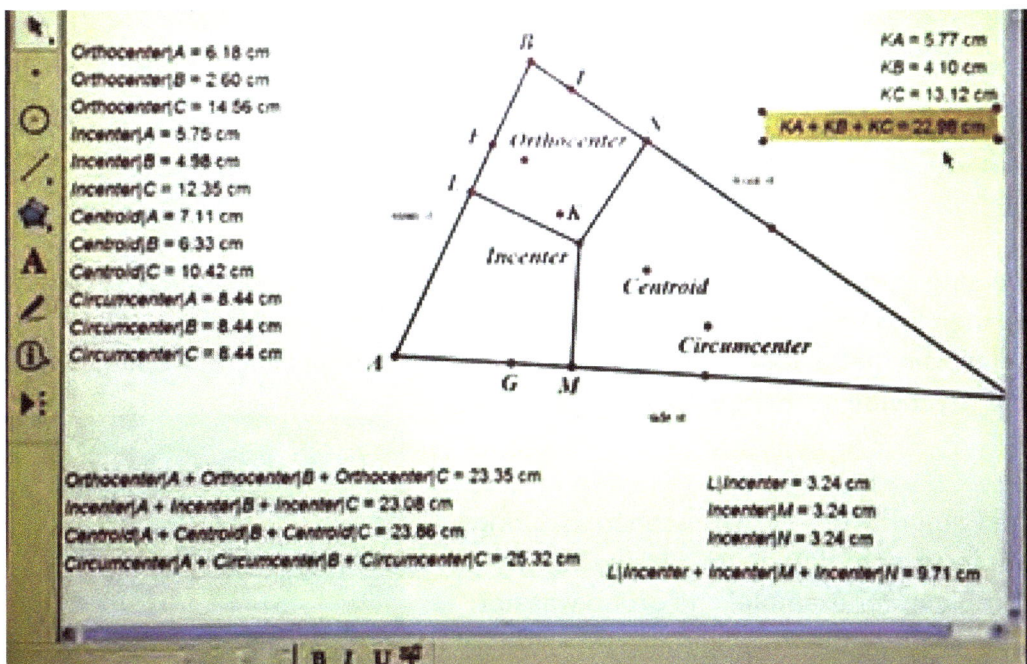

Final Presentation

All of the groups came to the same conclusion, that the incenter was the best place to build the shopping center. The incenter is the point out of the four centers examined that would result in the smallest sum of distances to the towns whether the roads are build directly to the towns (vertices of the triangle) or directly to the existing roads (sides of the triangle).

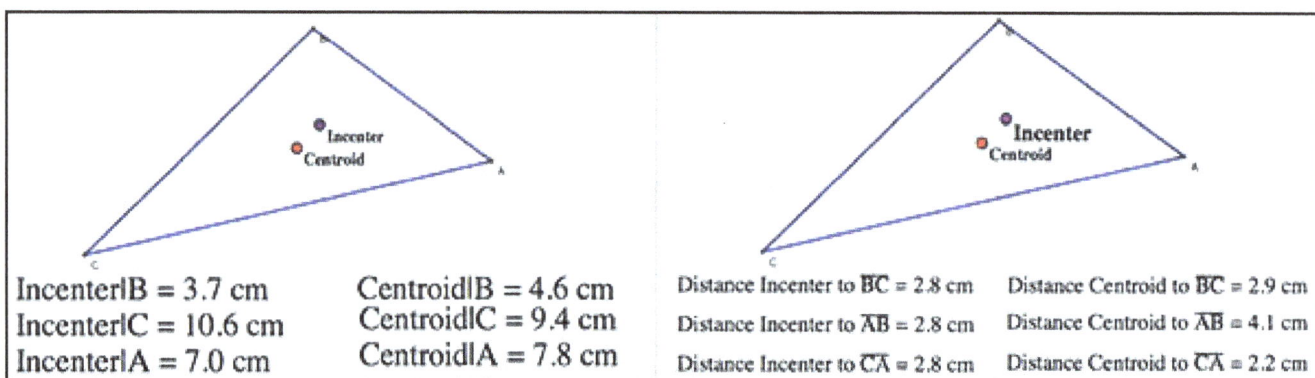

IncenterIB = 3.7 cm	CentroidIB = 4.6 cm	Distance Incenter to $\overline{BC}$ = 2.8 cm	Distance Centroid to $\overline{BC}$ = 2.9 cm
IncenterIC = 10.6 cm	CentroidIC = 9.4 cm	Distance Incenter to $\overline{AB}$ = 2.8 cm	Distance Centroid to $\overline{AB}$ = 4.1 cm
IncenterIA = 7.0 cm	CentroidIA = 7.8 cm	Distance Incenter to $\overline{CA}$ = 2.8 cm	Distance Centroid to $\overline{CA}$ = 2.2 cm

A Comparison of Incenter and Centroid

The next video shows part of a group's final presentation as they gave the rationale for the incenter.

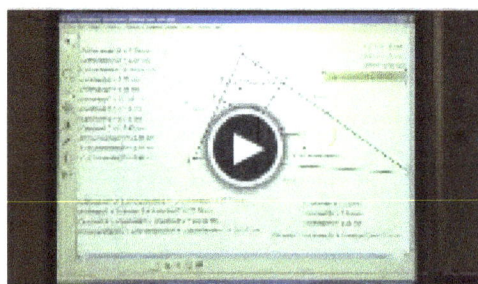

http://editlib.org/u/S_M_Video8

In addition to assessing student work during the investigation, student understanding was assessed as they presented their findings to the class. Students used the whiteboard to show their constructions and explain their findings. Each group not only had to give the reasoning behind the point selected, but to provide a rationale for the points that they rejected.

Nancee challenged groups with alternate scenarios during their presentations in order to determine how well they understood the problem. For example, one group was not allowed to build the roads to the existing roads (the sides of the triangles). In this case, they justified why the incenter was still the best solution.

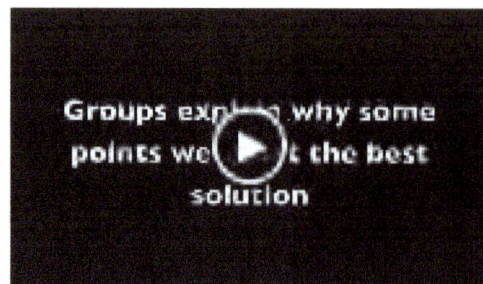

Groups explain why some points were not the best solution

http://editlib.org/u/S_M_Video9

What evidence do you see of students using their mathematical knowledge to solve meaningful problems?

How did Nancee use GSP as a tool to encourage her students to persevere when solving problems?

Teacher Reflection

It always feels like I run out of time. I wanted to explore some of the students' questions further, but I did not have the time. Most specifically, the random point that some pairs found that produced the smaller total sum of the lengths of the roads can be found systematically, and it is known as the Fermat point (when all angles are less than 120°). I was able to use Geometer's Sketchpad to show the students this point. I don't know how I would use an exploration like Building a Shopping Center if I didn't have the technology.

I also like how this activity allowed students to bring in their special knowledge. For example, one student had experience with surveying tools and repeatedly mentioned using a surveying tool called butterflies that could be used to locate our seemingly random point.

Interestingly, characteristics of the location of the shopping center that would serve the towns equally after the construction process were not discussed by any of the students, but the problem could have been expanded to include these constraints. For example, students could have considered that the shopping center needed to be built at a location equidistant from each town so that no town had a longer distance to travel.

How would you improve this activity or do it differently?

What other content could you use Geometer's Sketchpad for in your classroom and how?

How could technology tools such as a dynamic geometry environment help all students to engage in complex problem solving?

Resources

Common Core State Standards Initiative. (2014). High school: Geometry– Modeling with geometry. Retrieved from http://www.corestandards.org/Math/Content/HSG/MG/

International Society for Technology in Education. (2014) ISTE Standards. Retrieved from http://www.iste.org/STANDARDS

King, J., Orihuela, Y., & Robinson, E. (2010). Focus in high school mathematics: Reasoning and sense making in geometry. Reston, VA: National Council of Teachers of Mathematics.

Secondary Science (Physics)

Yash Patel | David Slykhuis | Tony Wayne

· · · Scenario · · · · · · · · · · · · · · · · · · ·

A bright red apple falling from a tree, an enormous rocket launching into space, a toddler jumping up and down in excitement, a bullet shot out of a rifle: What do all these things have in common? They are all affected by gravity.

The world has been fascinated with the role of gravity since the 16th and 17th century—the most formal experiments starting with Galileo dropping balls off the leaning tower of Pisa and continuing through the development of the complete theory of quantum gravity. The groundwork for gravitation was published by Isaac Newton in 1687 in his manuscript *Principia*, in which he hypothesized the inverse-square law of universal gravitation. Although Newton's theory has been superseded, most modern nonrelativistic gravitational calculations are still made using Newton's theory. It is much simpler in practical terms than Albert Einstein's theory of general relativity and gives sufficiently accurate results for objects with small masses, speeds, and energies.

So why does an apple fall down as opposed to falling up? With what force does it fall downward? How quickly does it accelerate? How fast is it going? How far away from the tree will it fall?

Think about a rocket breaking through the earth's atmosphere. How much force is needed to propel the rocket into outer space? Where will the rocket end up once the thrust is complete?

A similar thought process can be used to think about the bullet being fired from a gun: When would it fall to the ground if allowed to move through space without running into an obstacle?

These are the types of questions that can be answered with a basic background in Newton's laws of motion, gravity, and kinematics equations.

This teaching case presents a lesson from Tony Wayne's physics classroom, in which students used a high-speed digital camera and motion tracking software to learn about uniform acceleration due to gravity and its effects on position and velocity over time. Students also discovered how manipulation of launch angle affects the range of a projectile.

This case is an excellent example of constructivist learning, in which students create their own meaning of the target concept. Technology became a means by which the teacher shifted the crux of learning to the students.

More than any of the others in this book, this case focuses on the teacher's thinking process and the decisions that he made during the lesson and what they meant for the students. Though the lesson is student centered, it is made so by the teacher's knowledge of the pedagogical approaches that mesh well with the content and technology.

Gravity is a relatively abstract concept, one not easily grasped by students. As they mature, their understanding of gravity shifts from "things fall down" to "things fall toward the center of the Earth." The concept of gravity taught in middle school, high school, and college goes much further. According to the Physics Standards of Learning in Virginia (which is where this case was filmed), students are expected to learn how objects accelerate in free fall, why objects with different masses hit the ground at the same time, that gravity is a force that acts at a distance, that objects exert an equal and opposite force on each other, and that gravity and acceleration are equivalent as described in Einstein's theory.

Teachers can begin to help their students develop an understanding of gravity by debunking alternate conceptions about the functionality of gravity through scientific discovery and inquiry-based learning. For example, some students may come to the lesson thinking that gravity is related to movement, proximity to the Earth, or magnetic fields. Students may think that the weight of an object affects the amount of time it takes to reach the ground during freefall. They also may not understand the components of the acceleration and velocity vectors of a projectile on the way up, at the peak of its trajectory, and on the way down from that peak.

Teaching by telling is an ineffective mode of instruction for most students. Students must be intellectually active to develop a functional understanding of abstract concepts like this one. They need to participate in the process of constructing qualitative models that can help them understand relationships and differences among concepts (Tam, 2000).

A strong background in gravitational laws, kinematics, and the principles put forth by Isaac Newton over 300 years ago will provide students with logical thinking skills that pertain to working with abstract concepts. The Virginia standards outlined a set of instructional practices and knowledge that students should acquire.

PH.1   The student will plan and conduct investigations using experimental design and product design processes.

PH.2   The student will investigate and understand how to analyze and interpret data.

PH.5   The student will investigate and understand the interrelationships among mass, distance, force, and time through mathematical and experimental processes.

The Common Core State English Language Arts Standards for Science and Technical Subjects provide additional guidance on students' learning of gravity and kinematics:

Common Core: Integration of Knowledge and Ideas

- Integrate and evaluate multiple sources of information presented in diverse formats and media (e.g., quantitative data, video, multimedia) in order to address a question or solve a problem.
- Evaluate the hypotheses, data, analysis, and conclusions in a science or technical text, verifying the data when possible and corroborating or challenging conclusions with other sources of information.
- Synthesize information from a range of sources (e.g., texts, experiments, simulations) into a coherent understanding of a process, phenomenon, or concept, resolving conflicting information when possible.

Undoubtedly, physics instruction looks different from one classroom to the next; however, the outcome of those classrooms should be the same. According to the National Research Council (2012), students who have just completed a physics class should have a deep understanding of simple concepts and be able to transfer those concepts to the bigger picture.

All too often, teachers lecture about how to use formulas, resulting in students learning how to use physics without fully understanding the fundamental concepts. The result is that students' knowledge of physics concepts is more relative to their familiarity with the problem they are trying to solve rather than with a deep conceptual understanding of the overall topic. Instead, physics teachers should facilitate students' fluid understanding of physics concepts. This approach to learning is both more appropriate and more robust and gives students more hands-on opportunities to construct conceptual knowledge rather than merely memorizing formulas and equations that are applicable only in certain specific situations.

?

What experiences do you have with technology in learning physics as a student or as a teacher? Did you feel that the technology helped you learn? Why or why not?

Thinking back on these technology-related activities you experienced, what were some things you would change if you could?

Meet the Teacher

- Tony Wayne
- Physics Teacher
- Albemarle High School

I have been a physics teacher at Albemarle High School for the past 28 years. It is a large public high school (with a student population of approximately 1,800) serving grades 9-12 located in Albemarle County just outside of Charlottesville, Virginia. I am also the science

http://editlib.org/go/Sec_Sci_Video1

department chair and have taught some mathematics in the past. I have received teaching awards from the Virginia Association of Science Teachers and also the Red Apple Award for use of technology in the classroom.

The class in which this lesson takes place was an Honors Physics class comprised of 26 students–13 boys and 13 girls. Though the class was split equally by gender, the socioeconomic status of the students varied greatly. In any case, each student must have successfully completed Algebra II and received a recommendation from the previous science teacher to be enrolled in the class. There were no special needs students with an individualized education plan in the class.

My philosophy of teaching science, especially physics, involves using a multimodal approach to teaching. Learning does not occur through the use of one representation. Students need a visual to go along with written words and the verbal information I am giving to them. They also need to participate in group work to bounce ideas off each other and help each other learn in a community-style classroom. I like to combine group work with certain other aspects that also emphasize independent learning and do not foster dependence on the teacher. My goal is to be a facilitator. I provide all the resources that the students need to learn and teach the students how to use the resources independently.

http://editlib.org/go/Sec_Sci_Video2

With regard to teaching kinematics, acceleration due to gravity and Newton's laws of motion, students need to perform experiments. They need to collect and analyze data to understand how theory correlates with reality. Technology plays a big role in this, as specific software and hardware allows efficient collection and analysis of data, which provides students with quick feedback. Doing inquiry-based lab work allows students to build logical thinking skills that they can use to solve problems in any classroom or real-life situation.

The activity described in this case study was used as a keystone lesson in which students learned about acceleration due to gravity and the effect of an angle on a projectile. This lesson was part of a larger unit on kinematics, projectile motion and gravity. The overarching objective of this lesson was to encourage students to use analytical thinking skills and simple kinematics to determine the acceleration due to gravity.

The students relied on videos I had posted on YouTube (http://editlib.org/go/Sec_Sci_Video3) to help scaffold them through the process of working with the technology. I designed the experiment so students would not only understand the functionality of constant acceleration but also derive its effect on position and velocity over time. I was able to assess student understanding through informal questioning throughout the learning process and also through their results and conclusions documented in a summative lab report.

The lesson was split into two parts: A warm-up activity and a lab.

The Warmup

I reviewed the previous class period's homework activity with the students. It was a basic review of mathematics used in projectile motion. We discussed with students' real-life scenarios of projectile motion to give them a little more real-life context for the unit. Essentially, I approached the lesson in this manner to not only review past material but to engage students and give them a taste for what was to come. In a way, I primed the pump for the rest of the lesson. Here is an example of one the questions that we reviewed:

> Romeo was trying to get Juliet's attention by throwing a rock up to her balcony. Juliet's balcony is 4.00 meters above Romeo's release when he throws the rock. The balcony is, horizontally, 5.85 meters from Romeo. Romeo throws a small pebble at 15 m/s at an angle of 70.0° with the ground. Will the pebble land on Juliet's balcony or will it miss it?

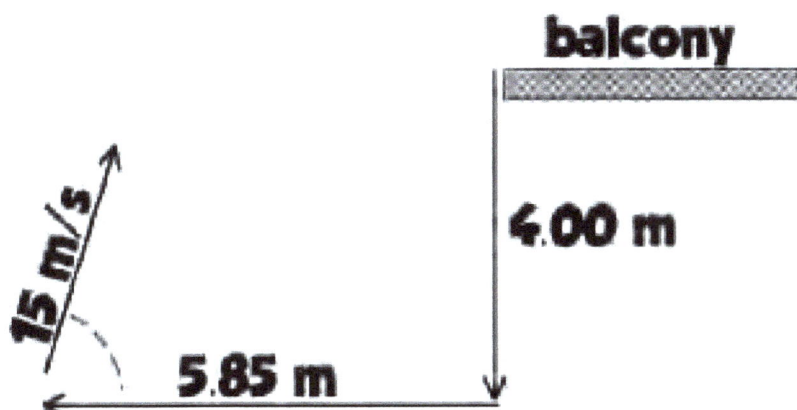

The warm-up activity set the tone for the rest of the class period. Students knew that they would be working with projectile motion, and I refocused their thinking on the use of proper equations in specific situations. After explaining to students that they would be doing an experiment, I worked with them on the proper use of the technology and began a short student-centered activity about which camera angles are most suitable for the experiment.

I divided the students into heterogenous ability groups of two or three with the goal of reviewing appropriate camera angles. We did not have enough cameras and whiteboards for students each to have their own. Given approximately 20 minutes, students were asked to work with their partners to determine why given camera angles were incorrect. The pictures they used were displayed on an interactive whiteboard, and they wrote their answers on their whiteboards to share with the rest of the class. After sharing with the class, the groups began to work with the camera and ball launcher set up to start the lab.

TPACK Commentary: Tony made an instructional choice to prepare students for the video analysis activity. While it may seem to be a trivial matter to film an object falling or in projectile motion, especially given today's students who are experienced taking both photographs and video, it is not. To ensure that a video can be analyzed, the object must move across the screen, the camera must be perpendicular to the motion, and the camera must be kept still. Additionally, the object needs to be clearly visible, and there needs to be an object in the frame of known length to set the scale. Tony designed this activity of viewing the pictures to identify incorrect camera set-ups and prepare the students to use the technology correctly. He thus ensured that the technology could fade to the background as much as possible and the lesson could remain focused on the physics content.

The Lab

The students began the lab portion of the lesson by returning to their groups and collecting the necessary materials as indicated on their lab worksheet - http://editlib.org/go/ProjectileLab.pdf). I showed a YouTube video that demonstrated to students how to work the cameras, which I had created in advance. I made several of these videos that could help with the technical portions of the experiment and posted them online. For example, my video that explains how import video into LoggerPro software and make a position vs. time graph can be viewed at http://editlib.org/go/Sec_Sci_Video4.

http://editlib.org/go/Sec_Sci_Video5a

The experiment included the use of several tools: (a) a high speed camera, (b) a ball launcher, (c) a ruler to use as a reference, (d) a paper box, and (e) a large clamp. The setup is illustrated in the graphic to the right.

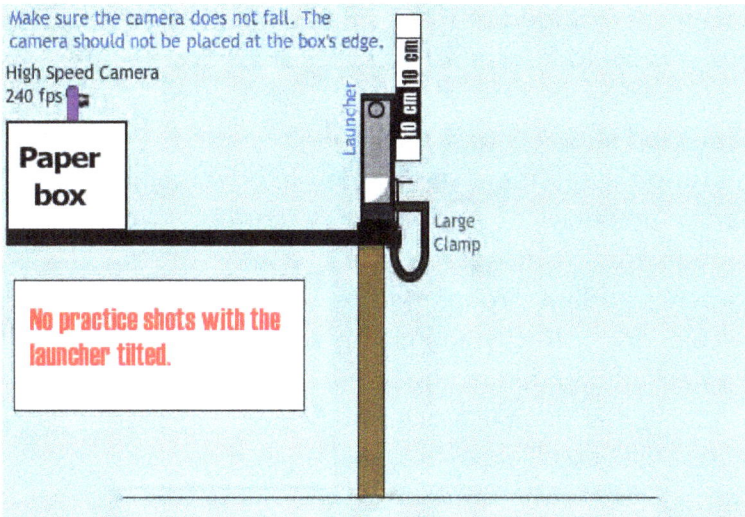

One student in each group was asked to work the launcher and the other to use the high speed camera to record the flight of the ball. The main objective of the lab was to predict where a projectile would land when launched at an angle from a ball launcher. This lab has two parts. In part 1, students calculated the initial velocity of the ball as it reached the end of a ramp. In part 2, students predicted where the ball would land and then got one launch to try to hit their predicted location.

In Part 1, students measured the average velocity of the ball for about the first 0.10 meters as it left the launcher. The launcher was set to the short range, and the ball was launched straight up. The digital camera recorded this event, and the video was transferred to the Vernier logger pro software. The students then used the video analysis software to determine initial velocity and acceleration, as illustrated in The Technology section of this case study.

In part 2, the students angled the ball launcher between 80 and 85 degrees from the normal. Based

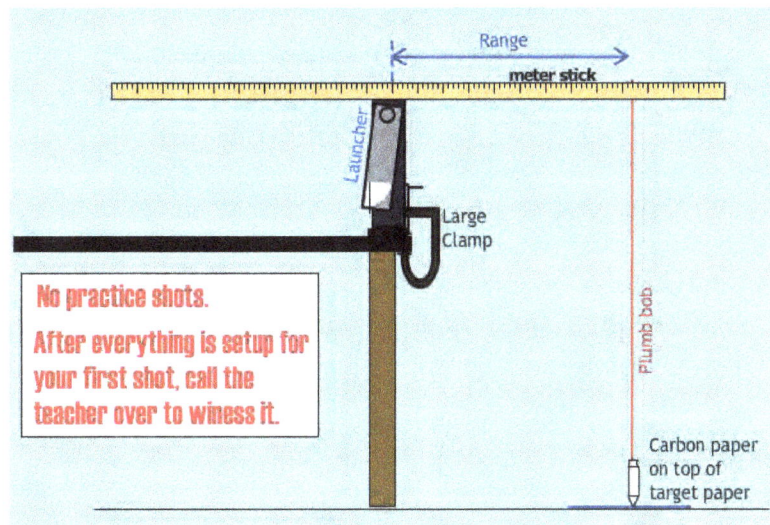

on the calculations from part 1, they were asked to predict where the ball would land.

On a piece of carbon paper, students marked where they thought the ball would land. After the launch, the ball made a mark on the paper where it landed. Using the carbon paper, students could trace exactly how far off they were with their predictions. Based on the data, students could then recalculate and reiterate quickly. Students called me over to witness whether they had accurately predicted where the ball would drop.

Students wrote up their lab reports in their groups on a document in Google Docs (which has been downloaded and is available as a pdf file - http://editlib.org/go/PhysicsLabWorksheet.pdf. The document included questions that students were required to answer. It was also formatted so that students could insert specific screenshots and pictures.

I assessed students based on their lab report. The lab report assessment was divided into two major parts, mastery of the physics content and experimental procedures. For mastery of the content, student groups had to show their final calculations correctly and clearly and evidence of their accuracy in hitting the target. To demonstrate proper experimental procedures student groups had to illustrate how they had cared for and properly put away equipment and made use of the videos as a resource instead of asking me questions.

http://editlib.org/go/Sec_Sci_Video5

TPACK Commentary: Tony's videos answered common questions and misconceptions about using the high speed cameras and associated software, allowing him to focus on pedagogy instead of the content. He freed himself during the face-to-face time with the students in the class to focus on their understanding of the physics, instead of spending his limited instruction time answering operational questions.

Using Google Drive to have the students work together to create a lab report for the group helped them focus on the physics content they learned for the day. He used technology in a way that enabled a high level of collaboration, as students worked in groups with shared responsibility making substantive decisions. Multiple students could write on the document and contribute ideas at the same time, which they could not have done with pencil and paper. This strategy also allowed for the extension of the learning opportunity beyond the classroom. If this assignment were completed with paper and pencil, only one student could have taken the report home after class, and collaboration would have ceased. Working online, most students continue to have access to the document and can use chat features to continue to discuss the content even when not physically together. In each of these instances the use of the technology was deliberate and an improvement over traditional methods not using technology.

The Technology

http://editlib.org/go/Sec_Sci_Video6

Students used a high-speed digital camera (taking 240 frames per second) and video analysis software (in this case, by Vernier) as they developed skills in kinematics equation analysis. The high-speed digital camera allowed students to document the process of construction equations in a way that a regular digital camera (30 frames per second) simply cannot. When shooting a video at a much higher frame rate, everything happens a lot slower. After students shoot a video and upload it to the Vernier software, they are able to break down even a quarter of a second into as many as 60 frames, in which the motion of the projectile can be tracked and subsequently analyzed.

Tony wanted students to know that what they were doing was grounded in the real world, which is why they made their own videos instead of watching premade videos. Students need to know that what they are doing is concrete, applicable, and relevant. A significant issue with technology such as probeware is called the "black box effect." Data and information are given to the students with limited understanding of where the data and information came from or how it was collected. With a lesson like this in physics, it is important

http://editlib.org/go/Sec_Sci_Video6a

for students to have a part in every single step, including the development of the videos. A premade video works just as well in analysis and drawing conclusions; however, the feeling of analyzing one's own work gives students more authority, initiative, and a sense that what they are dealing with is real and not somehow fabricated for easier data collection.

http://editlib.org/go/Sec_Sci_Video7

The video analysis software was used to determine the velocity and acceleration over time by marking the displacement of the projectile on each frame. Once the videos were made, students imported the video file in the software. The students then tracked the trajectory of the projectile frame by frame while using a reference scale in the background. Specifically, students included an embedded scale in each video that was then calibrated with the software.

In the example picture below, the scale is a meter stick marked by three blue strips. The meter stick tells the software exactly how long 1 meter is as a reference. Subsequently, students can move the video along frame-by-frame while marking the projectile's position in each frame (students can also skip frames as each frame denotes the passing of $1/240^{th}$ of one second). As this process unfolds, the software generates a graph of distance over time that can then be manipulated to generate velocity or acceleration graphs as a function of time.

This process allows students to determine velocity with respect to time for the x and y components of the object's motion independently. This technology gave students immediate feedback and reduced cognitive load by performing repetitive mathematical calculations. Students' working memory was freed up to focus on conceptual understanding and translating between data, the visual representation of video, the graphs, and the mathematics. This process allowed the students to take a very brief event, maybe a second or two of the ball in flight, and break it down precisely. By going through the video and marking the location of the ball on each frame, the students were aware of exactly how the data was collected.

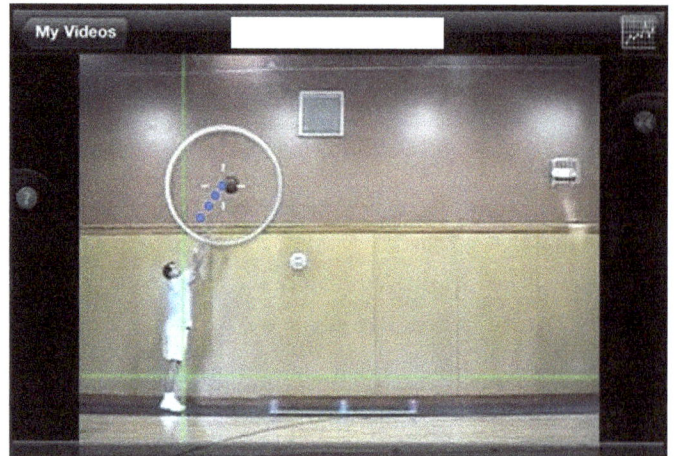

Once the position of the ball has been marked on all the frames and the graphs generated, students can play the event repeatedly and watch as the graph is created that represents the video event. Thus, the physical event and its graphical representation are linked in their minds. The students can focus on certain parts of the video to find critical pieces of information to solve the assigned problem, such as determining the velocity and acceleration the moment the ball leaves the launcher. They may also analyze interesting moments in the video that may or may not be part of the solution to their problem, such as what happens to the ball at the moment it reaches its peak height.

The use of the high-speed video camera and motion analysis software aligns with the following ISTE National Educational Technology Standards for Students (NETS-S).

   1c. Students use models and simulations to explore more complex systems and issues
   4c. Students collect and analyze data to identify solutions and/or make informed decisions

? What did the technology enable the students to do to help them better understand the concepts in the lab?

What black-box experiences still exist in this lab?

TPACK Commentary: One of the difficult things for students to do in physics class is to analyze motion in real time, as it happens very quickly. Tony knew that if this lab activity were to be completed without the technology, the students would have had two pieces of data: (a) initial time and (b) position and final time and position (and the final data would have been imprecise if measured with a stopwatch). The level of analysis that can be accomplished with those two points of data is limited. If the motion of the ball took 1.5 seconds, the high-speed camera turns those two data points into 360 data points. The video analysis software then takes those 360 data points and creates the x and y data, doubling the amount of data to 720 points. The computer turns the position data into velocity vs. time data (the first derivative) in both the x and y direction and into acceleration vs. time data (the second derivative) in both the x and y direction, giving students 2,880 points of data.

Tony chose to use the pedagogy of inquiry and the use of collaborative groups to best utilize this technology. Working together to solve a problem, predicting the landing point, the groups of students could analyze this abundance of data to come to a solution. Having multiple perspectives in their group forced students to defend and explain their conclusions, which led to a deeper understanding of the physics content. These explanations can be backed by the wealth of data the students collected using the software.

Classroom in Action

Inquiry and collaboration are significant themes throughout the activities that took place in this lesson. As you read through these vignettes and watch the videos, keep Tony's pedagogical approach in mind and think about how he took advantage of the affordances of the technology and prepared his students as creative and inquisitive learners.

Vignette 1

Watch the following video clip to see how Tony used images as part of an activity to check students understanding of the homework (watching some videos on the proper use of the cameras and software) that had been assigned in the previous class.

http://editlib.org/go/Sec_Sci_Video8

This activity is a check for understanding of the video assignment from the night before. Why did he use class time to go over this again? Why might students still not know everything they need to know about using the high-speed camera even after watching a video about it?

The online videos were used to teach about the high-speed cameras. While this is content, it is not physics content. What are the advantages of putting these camera-use directions in online videos?

TPACK Commentary: Operating a high-speed camera (or any new gadget, for that matter), can be overwhelming for a high school student who lacks experience with it. Tony had built in scaffolding by making digital videos that thoroughly explain the technical specifications of the high-speed camera relevant to the lab. He also demonstrated how to use the camera correctly and effectively. The students could pause and rewind the video as needed and did not need Tony at their side to help them work the camera. The warm-up activity allowed students to think critically and logically about camera positioning and angles and why this is critical to filming video that can be analyzed properly. The videos also explained the logistics involved with using the video analysis software.

Vignette 2

In this clip, Tony used video clips to instruct his students on how to manipulate the setting on the high speed camera to optimize them for use with the video analysis software.

http://editlib.org/go/Sec_Sci_Video9

? What are some advantages and disadvantages to giving the directions via video from both the students and teachers perspective?

Why did Tony want students to have the cameras in their hands as they watched his video?

TPACK Commentary: Many teachers experience the struggle with students following directions. Even when the directions are clearly written out on the lab, often student don't follow them or even read them. Tony used video to help solve this problem. He could make sure the video related the instructions to the students in a clear and concise manner. Also, students could refer to the directions as many times as they needed without having to interrupt instruction for other students by taking the teacher's time.

· · · Teacher Reflection ·

I believe that the lesson went really well and that the technology integration facilitated the lesson and scaffolded for the student activities as needed. We did run into a small problem – sometimes there is a problem with visual distortion on the camera lens, which skews the results. However, the in-class activity on camera angles that took place after the homework review gave students some ideas on how to eliminate the errors.

The technology use did not precipitate any classroom management issues. Since I am comfortable and have experience incorporating technology into my instruction, I was able to anticipate and prevent many problems. I provided pre-assessments with camera aspect problems that helped students learn the technology and provided instruction in both written and video form to facilitate for different types of learners. Also, the videos can be replayed or played back at a slower rate, making consumption of the material easier for the student.

This activity takes a lot of work to prepare. Student accountability takes trust and hard work to build over time. I recommend that any novice teacher do the lab before assigning it. Making a few videos that help students through the sticky or more-difficult portions of the lab is the most helpful thing for a novice teacher who is going to be crunched for time. In a class of diverse students, get to know the students' weaknesses and plan for them. You can't plan for everything, but the more you plan, the less you'll have to troubleshoot during actual class time, and the more you'll be able to facilitate conceptual understanding.

Resources

Common Core State Standards Initiative. (2014). English language arts standards for science and technical subjects: Grade 11-12. Retrieved from http://www.corestandards.org/ELA-Literacy/RST/11-12/

National Research Council. (2012). Discipline-based education research: Understanding and improving learning in undergraduate science and engineering. Washington, DC: National Academies Press.

Tam, M. (2000). Constructivism, instructional design, and technology: Implications for transforming distance learning. Educational Technology & Society, 3(2), 50-60.

Virginia Department of Education. (2003). Science standards of learning: Physical science. Retrieved from http://www.doe.virginia.gov/testing/sol/standards_docs/science/2003/index.shtml

Elementary Social Studies

Raina Kim | John K. Lee | Anna Isley

Interactive Activity

Before you begin the case study, please try the Interactive Visual Timeline by clicking on the image below. You should use your existing knowledge and the clue sheet (http://bit.ly/cluesheet) as a guide to placing pictures in proper chronological order. Spending a few minutes plotting the images will help you think about the skill and knowledge involved in using this online timeline tool.

The Interactive Visual Timeline

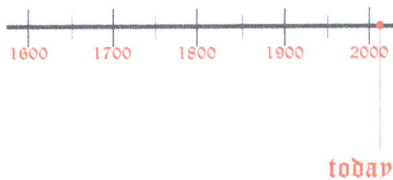

Click here to explore the Visual Timeline Tool (http://bit.ly/vistime)

What strategies and knowledge did you use to place the images on the timeline?

How might your approach differ from that of a third grade student?

Scenario

Timelines are an important pedagogical tool for social studies teachers. A well-constructed timeline can help students organize discrete content into recognizable patterns. Timelines structure the past by both sequencing and situating events in relation to one another. Recognizing these temporal relationships is critical for students to build their understanding of the past.

In some ways, the concept of sequencing, or what we call chronology, is easy for students to grasp. The most important operation in a chronology occurs when events are placed in the correct order. When provided with visual clues, young children can be quite adept at placing items in correct order. Children as young as kindergarten can use clues related to technology and style of dress to determine a chronology.

Students often have more trouble when trying to match an event or person to a specific date or period or when trying to use cause and effect to order events. For example, students may know that a picture of a covered wagon depicts an event that occurred before an event depicted in a photo with an automobile. Young children may even be able to correctly sequence an early model of the automobile and a current model. Those same children will likely find it more difficult to describe the date or period when the technologies were used. Students may also have trouble understanding that one event caused or led to another.

Making connections between events helps students to weave together a more coherent narrative of the past. For example, if students know that Beethoven wrote his famous Fifth Symphony at the same time as Lewis and Clark's exploration, they might have richer understanding of the differences between North America and Europe.

Timelines are a useful and tangible way to represent chronology and can help students to build sophistication with regard to the ordering of events. Perhaps more importantly, timelines can help students understand the distance between events or people in time and the commonalities between events that occur in the distant places.

In this chapter, Anna Isley describes her use of a timeline tool in her third-grade classroom. The tool is designed to support students in their development of chronological thinking and reasoning. In the instructional activity featured in this chapter, Anna wanted to help her students understand the relationships between 14 "Famous Americans" in history.

The social studies standards in Anna's state require the following of third graders:

Contributions of Citizens Who Defended American Principles:

> 3.11 The student will explain the importance of the basic principles that form the foundation of a republican form of government by identifying the contributions of George Washington, Thomas Jefferson, Abraham Lincoln, Rosa Parks, Thurgood Marshall, Martin Luther King, Jr., and Cesar Chavez... (Virginia Department of Education, 2008)

6-2

On Virginia's standardized test for third graders, students are expected to know all the famous Americans introduced in grades K-3. In addition, Anna reviewed seven historical figures students had learned about in prior grades. Anna used this new teaching opportunity to integrate students' prior learning with current learning, since many of the 14 historical figures had overlapping goals or were alive around the same time period.

At the end of the history unit on the contributions of these Famous Americans, Anna showed her students how to use an online timeline tool to help them place the historical figures in time in relation to each other and show chronological relationships among these people. This type of knowledge lays the foundation for the type of chronological thinking emphasized by the National Council for the Social Studies (2013) as students, "create and use a chronological sequence of related events to compare developments that happened at the same time" (C3 Framework, D2His. 1.3-5.).

The National Standards for History (Nash, 1996) also emphasize this sort of temporal thinking. Specifically, these standards expect of students that they will "interpret data presented in time lines and create time lines by designating appropriate equidistant intervals of time and recording events according to the temporal order in which they occurred" (Historical Thinking Standard 1, Standards for Grades K-4).

?

In what ways might young children struggle with chronological relationships between people and the events in history?

What kinds of strategies might you use to help students place significant people and events in their appropriate historical context?

Meet the Teacher ·

- Anna Isley
- 3rd Grade Teacher
- Burnley-Moran Elementary School

Currently, I am a third grade teacher at a school located in a small but culturally rich city surrounded by rural communities. Our school has nearly 400 students of whom nearly 50% receive free and reduced lunch. About half of the students are Caucasian, one third are African American, and the remaining students come from a variety of backgrounds - most of them ESL/ELL students. I have been teaching for seven years.

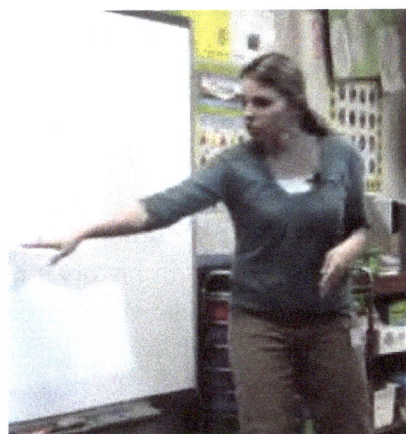

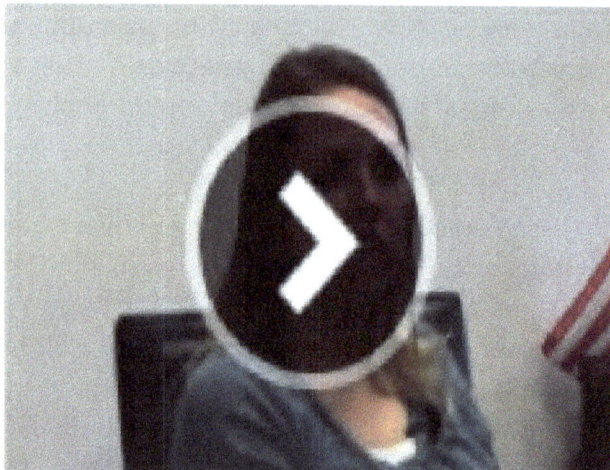

http://editlib.org/go/EL_SS_Video1

In teaching social studies, I use technology to help students understand the world in concrete ways. Examples of other technology tools we have used in this class include Google Earth to locate and see the ancient Greek ruins. I also have plans to use videoconferencing (Skype) to connect the students to another classroom in a different country. I believe it is critical for my students to build critical thinking and reasoning skills in addition to learning the facts. Also, I want them to be comfortable using different technologies, since using technology is an important 21st-century skill they will need.

My third-grade class includes a diverse group of students. They differ in terms of where they are developmentally, their academic performance, their ability to express themselves, and their physical capacity. This lesson does not hinge on perfect recall or performance; it allows students to make mistakes, use their own reasoning and judgment, and work collaboratively.

The Activity

Often, students in the third grade who learn facts about important events and people have a hard time organizing their relative positions in time. My goal for the digital timeline lesson was to encourage students to use critical thinking and reasoning skills to determine the position of each historical figure on the span of time, understand how these historical figures are related to one another, and demonstrate and articulate their thinking. (Watch the video for more about Anna's philosophy on teaching this topic.)

My students had studied the facts about what we refer to in our state standards as the Famous Americans and their contributions to history. In a related math lesson, the students learned how to determine the lifespan of each of the Famous Americans and plot their birth and death years on a number line. These previous lessons provided the context and background knowledge from which students could draw and extend for this lesson.

Knowledge and skill alone, however, do not help the students conceptualize passing of time, the sequence of events in history, and the resulting relative positions of people and events in history. Students need to use their knowledge and reasoning skills to make sense of how people and events fit together.

As I introduced the lesson, the students were seated in groups and given a laptop with the browser open. I knew these students were fairly comfortable with using laptops, so I didn't need to teach any computer skills or competencies in order for them to participate in the lesson.

The browser had two tabs, one with the timeline and one with the clues sheet. I modeled how students could work with the tool and reason out their answers before getting them started on the group work.

Prior to the lesson, I had added 14 images of Famous Americans on the left side of the screen. On the right was a timeline beginning just before 1600 CE and ending just past 2010. Each century was marked with the year and the mid-century was noted with a short line. The only other marker on the timeline was "Today" to indicate that the current year belongs on the timeline.

The challenge was for students to drag each image from the left side of the screen to a correct approximate position on the timeline. They were also to discuss with a partner their reasoning for putting these people on the timeline in a particular spot, using their knowledge of the ideas and values of these historical figures and their contributions to society and history.

At the end of the lesson, I asked students to share their strategies so they could learn about strategies their classmates used. I emphasized that placing the images precisely where they belonged was less important than using their background knowledge to reason where they would logically go.

?

What prerequisite content knowledge would your students need for this activity?

What are some of the possible issues that may occur with students working with computers in groups and how could a teacher attempt to minimize those issues in advance?

The Technology

In this lesson, Anna chose to use an online timeline tool, the Interactive Visual Timeline, developed specifically for this video case. There are a number of other Web-based timeline tools that you might also use that include additional features. For example, Timeliner XE® is a robust software-based tool. TimeToast and Dipity are nice Web-based alternatives.

The Interactive Visual Timeline enabled Anna to add photos of the historical figures she expected her third-grade students to know. It provides a timeline that extends between 1600 CE and the present, with each century labeled and mid-centuries marked. Students drag the images to the

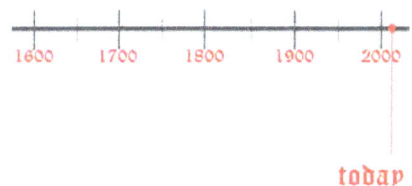

place in time where they judge they belong.

The tool is web based and contains a minimal number of features, so it could be implemented without much scaffolding. The lack of specificity in increments of the timeline is an important feature. It allows younger students to focus on relative placement and general understanding. Also, the lack of specific dates on the timeline and in the requirements of the assignment helps target critical thinking over a focus on specific dates. Watch the video to hear Anna talk about why she likes to use the Interactive Visual Timeline.

http://editlib.org/go/EL_SS_Video2

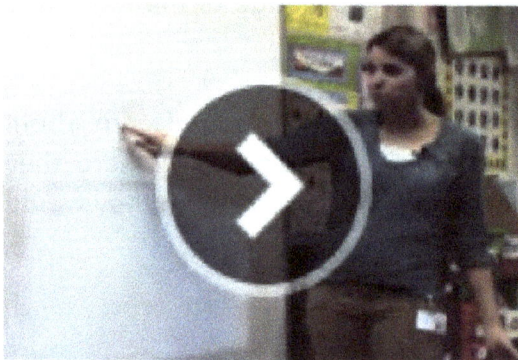

http://editlib.org/go/EL_SS_Video3

In this video, notice how Anna prepared her students to effectively use the timeline tool. Try to identify techniques that reveal her technological pedagogical content knowledge in action.

TPACK Commentary: In selecting the visual timeline tool, Anna focused on the pedagogical advantages of the approach. She highlighted the ability for students to easily manipulate the positioning of the different images on the timeline. She made special note of how easy it is for students to change the positioning – offering an easy way for students to experiment and try out new sequences. This focus on the pedagogical affordances or advantages of using a technology tool in the classroom is often the motivating factor for teachers to use a tool in their teaching.

In recognizing that she would need to model and clearly explain what the students would be doing with the timeline, Anna drew on her knowledge of effective teaching with technology. By highlighting the features of the timeline and the clue sheet and demonstrating how students should use the features, Anna provided students with a model for their work.

TPACK Commentary (continued): Anna told the students that they would not be placing people exactly on dates, but rather that they should focus on their relative positions based on what they knew and could infer from the images. She established learning goals and set clear expectations for a process to reach these goals. By modeling how students could arrive at a solution before getting them started on the group work, Anna helped focus students on the content and cognitive task at hand, as opposed to focusing on the technology.

Anna identified a problem with her students' understanding of chronology. Students were able to put things in order, but had a difficult time understanding differences in the amount of time between events and the concept of "long ago." This ability to predict common student challenges or misconceptions related to the content is an aspect of her pedagogical content knowledge (PCK). She brought in her technological knowledge of the timeline to extend her PCK thinking.

The timeline tool enabled students to place people on the timeline and visually depict the distance in time that existed between these individuals' lives. These experiences were powerful enough to justify the use of this timeline tool. This sort of reasoning is central to TPACK, as teachers make decisions about whether to use technologies and how those technologies will support students' learning.

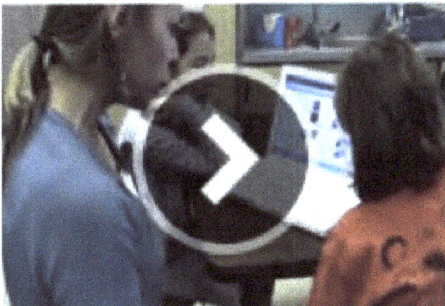

As you watch this video, try to identify ways Anna used her questioning skills to elicit students' reasoning for their timeline choices.

The following two videos show additional examples of Anna working with student pairs on the timeline. Note the ways she uses questions and hints to guide her students.

http://editlib.org/go/EL_SS_Video4

http://editlib.org/go/EL_SS_Video5

http://editlib.org/go/EL_SS_Video6

? Why do you think Anna opted for a less feature-rich timeline tool rather than a more sophisticated one? What do you see as advantages and disadvantages of this instructional decision?

Give two examples of ways Anna supported the students' articulations of their reasoning and idea construction?

TPACK Commentary: Notice that Anna's conversations with the students did not focus upon the tool but rather their reasoning process in placing the images on the timeline. The tool helped to set up and facilitate deeper conversations about the content. In this way we see that the technology is a tool that supports the primary learning objective of students applying their chronological reasoning skills.

Anna didn't merely sit at her desk while student groups were working. She walked around and observed students' progress, stopping to interject questions when she thought students needed help with articulating their thinking. The timeline tool encouraged the students to collaborate on decisions about where to place their images of historical figures. Anna knew that the flexibility of this tool would support communication between students, since each can take turns moving an image easily along the timeline. When students disagreed, they could adjust the placement of image, defend their decision and then listen to other students' responses.

In order to help students practice their chronological reasoning, Anna allowed students to work with historical figures that they had recently learned about in her class. She wanted to limit the amount of new learning so students could focus on the chronological thinking concepts supported by the tool. Anna also had students work in groups so they could support one another in the activity. Video 3 is a great example of this kind of collaborative thinking. She tried to offset some of the potential complexities in navigating the tool by carefully instructing students about how to use the tool in their web browser.

The technology played a direct role in supporting students' development of conceptual knowledge about ordering, time scales, and causation. During the debriefing, Anna drew on students' experiences using the timeline tool to further expand their conceptual knowledge.

As Anna walked around, she assessed students' progress. At the end of the lesson she asked students to share their strategies. She chose to conclude the activity with a discussion of the strategies students used to arrive at their answers. Watch the videos of some of her concluding interactions with students.

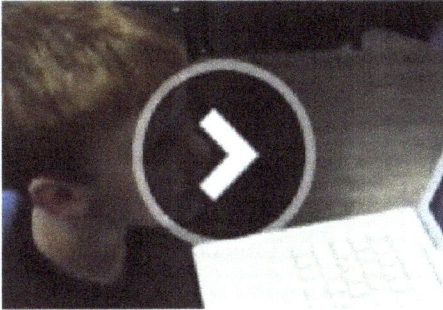

http://editlib.org/go/EL_SS_Video7

http://editlib.org/go/EL_SS_Video8

Do you think Anna's choice of assessment strategies in the lesson was effective? Why or why not? What might you do differently?

TPACK Commentary: The technology Anna used for this lesson allowed her students to explore content in new ways. Specifically, the technology helped students manipulate historical information so they could understand temporal concepts such as before, after, and long ago. She also wanted to help students understand the temporal context of historical causation, in other words, how one thing causes or leads to another. Anna emphasized that the closer events or people were on the timeline, the more likely one had an effect on the other.

One major strength of this lesson is the clear focus. Beginning with the modeling at the start of the lesson all the way through the debrief at the end, Anna focused on helping her students develop their reasoning skills. Her TPACK reasoning allowed her to select pedagogical strategies that took advantage of the timeline tool to help her students develop these key understandings.

The timeline tool helped students apply the historical content they learned in the context of time. Up to now, they had learned pieces of information that, on their own, do not translate to practical understanding. For example, the mathematics activity of subtracting the year born from the year of death of the Famous Americans helped students learn to use a number line and plot points and duration. We know that the students will forget most of those dates. However, even after they forget the dates, I think these students will now be able to reason their way through understanding when one person's important role in history was influenced by another person's accomplishments, or if multiple people during an era all worked toward similar goals. (Watch the video for additional reflection by Anna on this lesson.)

I didn't experience many problems with students being off task while working with the timeline tool. I monitored them by periodically scanning the room. I was able to gain a basic understanding of which students needed the most support by simply glancing at computer screens and noting how many images were already placed. For students who quickly placed their photographs, I wanted them to be able to defend their choices and think creatively about how they could decide where historical figures should go relative to others and not merely memorize the years they were alive. For other students, I asked more basic questions to help them place some anchor people they could use as comparisons for the remainder of the photos. I asked, "Who was the first person we learned about?" or "Who was our first president?"

In terms of time, my students know that the goal is not always to have everything totally complete but rather to understand and to explain what they did complete. Those few who hadn't placed every single photo did not stress about not having them all in place. Most students completed the task quite efficiently, though.

One way to alter the lesson if students were not as successful would be to give the student partners time on their own and then bring everyone back and have a more whole-group discussion in which students could share strategies and thinking while we complete the time line together. I would definitely make an alteration in the lesson such as this if I saw that the majority of students were struggling to grasp the activity.

http://editlib.org/go/EL_SS_Video9

In the future I would include primary sources in addition to photographs with this lesson. For example, I might include a suffragist's sign for women's rights or a copy of the Declaration of Independence or a freedom song from the civil rights era. In this way, students would have to apply even more of their critical thinking skills. Not only would they need to synthesize information from a variety of lessons about the Famous Americans, but they would need to read and analyze primary source documents and infer where these would fit in based on context clues. Such sources would be new to students and could not be accessed and placed simply by memory alone. Likely, adding additional sources would increase the dialog and debate between student pairs as well.

? If you were to use this tool in your classroom, how might you approach the process differently? Why?

Resources

Nash, G. B. (1996.) *National standards for history: Basic edition*. Los Angeles, CA: National Center for History in the Schools.

National Council for the Social Studies. (2013). College, career, and civic life (C3) framework for social studies state standards. Retrieved from http://www.socialstudies.org/c3

Virginia Department of Education. (2008). History and social science standards of learning: Enhanced scope and sequence: Grade 3. Retrieved from the VDOE Standards of learning Website: http://www.doe.virginia.gov/testing/sol/standards_docs/history_socialscience/

The authors would like to express gratitude to the following people among the many who have contributed their time to the case study: Laurel Gillette, Bill Ferster, Melanie Bowyer, Willy Kjellstrom, Emily Furnari, and Bert Jacoby.

Secondary Social Studies

John K. Lee | Andrea Gambino Rhodes

Scenario

Globalization is an increasingly important content area in social studies. Content is a central part of most world history, world studies, and geography curricula. As important as globalization is in social studies, it is equally difficult to teach. The content is complex, resources are hard to come by, and the products of students' learning require creative planning. The strategic application of technology can ease these constraints. Web-based content creation tools are particularly useful in distributing student work and for developing products of students' learning. In this case, Andrea Gambino Rhodes describes her use of several web-based content creation tools to support a project-based learning unit that she facilitated in her seventh-grade world history classes on the modern era of globalization.

In order to better understand how Andrea used the technology, it is important to understand what globalization is and why it can be hard to teach. Globalization can be described as the events and processes by which local economic, social, cultural, and political systems are being integrated into globally interdependent systems. The modern era of globalization began after World War II with the establishment of the United Nations. Over the last six decades, the development of multinational corporations, the rapid expansion of air travel, and the development of cheap and reliable communications systems have fueled globalization.

Because globalization is a modern and even emerging concept, finding print resources on this topic can be difficult. Lecture and direct instruction do not work well, because of the complexity of the content. Project-based learning (PBL) is a particularly useful method for teaching about globalization. Through PBL, teachers can engage students in authentic and rigorous globalization content. In PBL, students can research complex globalization questions or problems for which they have some interest and create products of their research that reflect what they have learned.

Although PBL is a good method for teaching about globalization, social studies teachers face a number of obstacles when utilizing the PBL approach. Chief among those issues are constraints on time given the breadth of the curriculum, the availability of content-related resources, and the means to support the preparation and presentation of student products.

This case describes how Andrea dealt with these challenges and how she applied her TPACK to facilitate her students' learning about globalization. Andrea aligned her unit with North Carolina's Essential Standards for Social Studies, the Common Core Standards for Literacy in History / Social Studies, and the C3 Framework for State Standards in Social Studies.

- North Carolina Essential Standards for seventh grade
  (http://www.ncpublicschools.org/docs/acre/standards/new-standards/social-studies/7.pdf)

  ○ H. 2: Understand the implications of global interactions.

- Common Core Standards for History / Social Studies in Reading and Writing
  (http://www.corestandards.org/ELA-Literacy/WHST/6-8)

  ○ CCSS.ELA-Literacy.WHST.6-8.6 Use technology, including the Internet, to produce and publish writing and present the relationships between information and ideas clearly and efficiently.

  ○ CCSS.ELA-Literacy.WHST.6-8.7 Conduct short research projects to answer a question (including a self-generated question), drawing on several sources and generating additional related, focused questions that allow for multiple avenues of exploration.

- C3 Framework for State Standards in Social Studies
  (http://www.socialstudies.org/system/files/c3/C3-Framework-for-Social-Studies.pdf)

  ○ D4.3.6-8. Present adaptations of arguments and explanations on topics of interest to others to reach audiences and venues outside the classroom using print and oral technologies (e.g., posters, essays, letters, debates, speeches, reports, maps) and digital technologies (e.g., Internet, social media, digital documentary).

? What technology tools are you familiar with that might facilitate student learning in a PBL environment?

Meet the Teacher

- Andrea Gambino Rhodes
- 7th Grade Social Studies Teacher
- Centennial Campus Magnet Middle School

Our school's magnet theme revolves around three areas: STEM, a partnership with a local university, and leadership, with a strong focus on character education guided by Stephen Covey's *Seven Habits of Highly Effective People.*

As a 1:1 school where every seventh and eighth grader has a laptop for use in every class, the school provides opportunities for students to have hands-on learning with emerging technologies. Our student population is about 625 students, and 41% of our students receive free and reduced lunch. As part of a smaller school environment we strive to individualize and differentiate instruction to meet the diverse needs of our students.

Teaching social studies has helped me gain perspective about our world. I believe social studies provides students with a unique opportunity to raise their awareness about culture, the world, and the beauty in the diversity of the world's people. I love seeing my students explore new ideas, environments, places, and regions.

I strongly believe that it is important to infuse daily instruction with the purposeful use of technology to prepare 21st-century learners and leaders. Through the careful and strategic use of technology in my instruction, I believe I can enhance my students' literacies, workplace skills, and levels of engagement with academic content. I hope that students will become passionate lifelong learners who understand how they can participate in our global society.

(Watch the video on the next page to learn more about Andrea's philosophy of using technology in 1:1 laptop program.)

http://editlib.org/go/Sec_SS_Video1

I focus instruction in my seventh-grade classroom on opportunities to conduct project-based learning (PBL). I find that technology can support PBL in that it enables my students to access information and to present and share the findings of their inquiry with others. Ultimately, I want my students to know that they are in a democratic environment that nurtures, respects, and values their individuality.

The Technology

Andrea used a whole suite of technologies in her unit on globalization – both in terms of organizing instruction and offering opportunities for students to share their understanding. She used Blackboard to stage all of the activities in the unit. Students accessed information on Blackboard (blackboard.com) about various activities, as well as links and support materials that they would need as they conducted their inquiries. Angela also used Blackboard as a presentation tool to set up activities and show students examples of the tools and sources they were using in their inquiries.

Students used a wide variety of technology tools to create the unit products, including Voicethread (voicethread.com) for creating presentations with video and audio files and Glogster (edu.glogster.com), an interface for mixing text, audio, video, images, graphics and data. Smore (smore.com) proved to be a useful way to design brief informational flyers about what students were learning. Photopeach (Photopeach .com) was a useful tool for students to organize visual content. Live Binder (Livebinder.com) allowed students to organize their work and store information for the duration of the inquiry. Each of these tools provided Andrea with something unique in her effort to support her students' inquiries.

One of the most important technologies students used was Weebly (weebly.com). It provided students a user-friendly platform to creatively design and share their work. Weebly is a web-authoring tool that includes simple-to-use templates for designing a multilayered website. The Weebly environment was

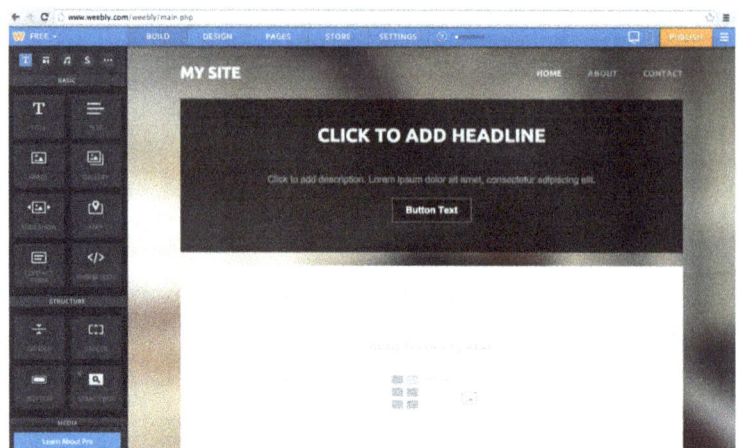

flexible enough to support all the text, videos, images, and illustrations that students created during their unit-long inquiries.

Click the link to the video at right to learn more about why Andrea chose Weebly for bringing together student projects.

The Weebly site allowed students to embed content into the websites they were creating. Students were able to organize findings, write reflections, and use a wide variety of images and video to enrich their work.

http://editlib.org/go/Sec_SS_Video2

Weebly supported students develop their multimodal skills. Instead of students presenting only to the teacher and their classmates, they were able to share their work across the grade level, the school, and even to online communities outside the school.

Students enjoyed having the flexibility to design their final Weebly projects using the layout options and other features available. Andrea often challenged students to push beyond what they were familiar with when designing their website.

? What kinds of insight into students' learning needs did Andrea consider as she developed this activity that was so rich with technology applications?

What other technology tools are you familiar with that might serve the same functions as those Andrea selected?

TPACK Commentary: Social studies is a complex subject area with multiple disciplines and a wide range of source materials. Inquiries in social studies often focus on current problems, and even when focusing on historical topics, teachers should aim to help students to apply what they are learning. Given the nature of social studies, the strategic use of technologies is vital. Students need to use technologies to access content and sources and to access each other. The skills they learn through the use of technologies are critical for civic democratic life.

In particular, the concept of globalization is particularly well-suited for multimedia. Globalization is a 21st-century concept and, thus, the source material students must access to understand more about the concept is also 21st century and in multimedia form (print, video, and images). Andrea knew that Weebly would enable students to share their work, going public in ways that closely connect to the concept of globalization. After all, the concept of globalization includes the idea that communication technologies have enabled people to share more and know more about one another than ever before. Technologies such as Weebly that enable sharing across physical borders are actually the product of globalization.

The Activity

This lesson was one of several activities in a project-based inquiry unit on globalization, which I designed in collaboration with my content professional learning team partner, Ryan Millhoff. The inquiry that students pursued focused on the question, "How does globalization influence people around the world?"

As a whole class, students selected global issues facing people in four countries or regions—Central Africa, China, The Middle East, and the United States. Working in groups, students then crafted compelling questions focused on each of these regions in succession. For one week, the groups focused on Central Africa, the next week China, the Middle East, and finally, the United States. In each of these regional units, students conducted research on specific global issues and created products of their work using various Web-based content creation tools. As a culminating experience, students brought all of their work together in an online multimedia portfolio of their learning using Weebly.

The lesson featured in this case focused on students designing products from their inquiries about global issues in China. At this point in the unit, students had completed one of the four successive inquires, so they had some understanding of how to use tools for research and to prepare products from their first inquiry on Central Africa. Students selected three issues – human rights (one-child policy), censorship, and pollution. The lesson featured here lasted 45 minutes and included the following activities.

1. An opening review of the group work – 10 minutes

2. Three successive group sessions focused on using technology tools to support the development of products – 10 minutes each, 30 minutes total

3. Concluding comments – 5 minutes

I facilitated discussions with each group about how they would use specific technology tools to create a product of their learning. In this lesson, students used a specific Web 2.0 tool in each group. Students were grouped based on the content topic, and each group used one tool to fit with their content. During this discussion, I facilitated students as they reviewed their content, monitored their progress using a checklist and began the process of developing a product of what they were learning. The tools were selected to support the students in the groups to complete their project work.

- The group working on human rights (one child policy) used a tool for making flyers called Smore (https://www.smore.com).

- The groups working on the censorship topic used the slideshow tool Photopeach (http://photopeach.com)

- The pollution group used Live Binder, a tool for organizing information online (http://www.livebinders.com)

I facilitated all of the groups as they worked with the information they were collecting from their research to start the process of developing products of their learning. This involved both reviewing content and introducing the technology tools. I worked with each group for about 10 minutes to accomplish both of these tasks.

To assess this unit, I took into account all aspects of students' work. Students engaged in a lengthy research process. They created written responses to the research questions and multimedia products on Weebly. Students also reflected on globalization issues and their role as global citizens. As a culminating activity, students prepared what we called a "Globalization Gala." During the gala, students presented their online products to sixth graders to help create awareness among the students about global issues and their responsibility as citizens to take an active role in society.

In all, there were five aspects I had to assess.

1. The research process.

2. Students' written responses to the inquiry questions.

3. Students' online portfolios.

4. Student reflections.

5. Students' presentation and interaction with their sixth-grade peers.

I used rubrics to access each of these activities. My assessment include scores on the rubrics, written feedback, and student interviews that I conducted to provide students opportunities to discuss global issues and reflect on how these projects affected their role as a global citizen.

Classroom in Action

In this first video, Andrea takes advantage of Blackboard to organize the various student project assignments in her China unit. Pay attention to ways she incorporated Blackboard in her introduction to the unit and provided advance organizers of the project.

http://editlib.org/go/Sec_SS_Video3

TPACK Commentary: Andrea was careful in this teaching episode to provide her students multiple channels of information about the tasks that they had to complete. She described each task, displayed them on a screen in the front of the room, and had students log into Blackboard to view the information on their computer screens. One of the most challenging aspects of facilitating project-based inquiry is managing the various directions that the PBLs are likely to go. This management problem is compounded when using a variety of technologies, as Andrea did. By using Blackboard, Andrea was able to deliver a well-paced and consistent message about the logistics of students' work, without distracting them or losing time. In this clip, Andrea explained the complex and distinct processes students would use in their PBLs in just 2 minutes, 30 seconds. This technology-aided efficiency maximized students' time to conduct research, and freed Andrea up to provide individual support.

http://editlib.org/go/Sec_SS_Video4

As you watch these next two videos, identify ways that Andrea wove together students' experiences with content and with learning new technologies. Think about her instructional approach for managing these experiences.

In the video at left, Andrea asks students to begin their work with three new web tools – Smore, Livebinder, and Photopeach. She wants students to "play to learn" as they start the process of creating the products of their inquiry. Consider the following questions as you watch this clip.

? Why do you think Andrea wanted her students to "play" with the technology tools as an initial activity?

How did Andrea weave together her instruction supporting students' content knowledge and their learning new technology tools?

In the next video, Andrea shifts her focus to working with individual groups. As the focus shifts, Andrea begins to attend to the specific content related to students' inquiries. The interplay between Andrea's talk about content and technology is dynamic and fluid. She moves from content to technology seamlessly in this clip. Consider the following questions as you watch this clip.

http://editlib.org/go/Sec_SS_Video5

? How did Andrea weave in discussions about content as she supported the groups in their work?

How did Andrea get students' attention away from the laptops when she needed them to go on to the next stage of the assignment? How might she have been more effective at this?

How did the technology that students used fit with the content?

TPACK Commentary: Andrea's decision to use web-based creation tools enabled her students to focus on their research and their emerging conclusions using tools that were suited for the products she envisioned from students' work. Because these Web 2.0 tools were designed to be user friendly, Andrea was able to give more time and attention to helping her students navigate the complexities of the globalization content, as opposed to technology troubleshooting as they designed their projects. By using a variety of tools Andrea was able to differentiate her instruction to meet individual students' needs.

She was successful because of the unique combination of the globalization content, the project-based inquiry pedagogy, and the Web 2.0 technologies. This is a classic example of TPACK in practice. The technology afforded or made possible instructional goals that were directly connected to academic content. Students were able to design products that represented what students were learning using the Web 2.0 tools, thus putting into practice a central tenant of globalization, which holds that communication technologies enable a merging of social, political, and economic systems.

Student Work

Ultimately, students brought together their work on the China inquiry with their work from inquiries on Central America, Africa and the United States. They created group Weebly sites to present what they learned about globalization and the various issues they were investigating. Students describe their work products in the following video clip.

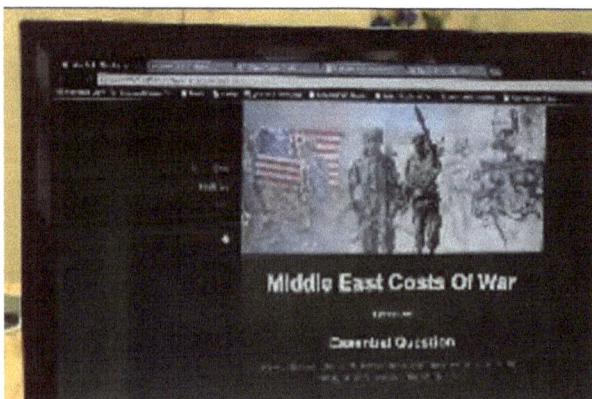

http://editlib.org/go/Sec_SS_Video6

Following are screenshots of two student Weebly sites. The entire collection of Weebly sites is available at http://centennialcampussocialstudies.weebly.com/

What evidence of student learning do you observe in this student work?

How might the technology tools have contributed to helping Andrea see what her students learned?

TPACK Commentary: Since students were actively involved in the learning process and using the creative design environment of the various Web tools, truly interesting learning was possible. By providing a democratic environment for active learning, students were able to take control of their own learning and were proud of the things they created. Students were able to demonstrate an understanding of the content issues they were exploring and were able to make use of technologies to organize and share what they learned.

Andrea's use of a variety of Web 2.0 tools and then using Weebly for the culminating project was designed to expand the reach of her students in communicating the results of their research. Far too often, teachers using PBL fail to include a process for communicating the results of student research. Similarly, teachers often do not provide students with opportunities to think about how they can take informed action on what they have learned.

In this case, Andrea tackled both of these issues, and technology played an important role in that process. Andrea enabled her students to act on what they learned by having them share with their sixth-grade peers. She created an environment where her seventh-grade students felt a responsibility to help educate their younger peers about important global issues. The Weebly technology supported this work by providing a platform for students to share their work with others. Students were able to share their work with people outside their school. In fact, you even now have access!

Teacher Reflection

Given the complexity of globalization and the wide range of ability levels in my classroom, it was often a challenge to find a way to reach everyone. I wanted to structure my students' uses of Web 2.0 tools so they were able to communicate information about what they were learning in such a way so as to not let the technology get in the way. Ultimately, I wanted the technology to be transparent.

I found that online design tools such Weebly had broad appeal for my students. At the same time, I had to be careful to manage my students as they developed their projects. Having this many students working on different websites was a challenge. I used two strategies to help manage the process. First, I had a series of regular progress checks where students were required to meet certain requirements in order to move to next step. The last of these progress checks is described in this case. My second strategy was to interview all students about their progress. I did this over the course of several days, and was able to provide important formative feedback to students on their learning and the development of their Weebly sites.

I thoroughly enjoyed learning about globalization alongside my students. I was able to witness firsthand the creativity that can occur when students are given the right kind of tools to support their learning. I thought my students found their voices and their purpose as active global citizens in this

?

What are some challenges that you foresee encountering in your own classroom when utilizing multiple technologies?

In what ways would you use technology differently or the same as Andrea did in her teaching?

Resources

National Council for the Social Studies. (2013). College, career, and civic life (C3) framework for social studies state standards. Retrieved from http://www.socialstudies.org/c3

Developing TPACK with Learning Activity Types

Mark Hofer | Judi Harris

Having explored several cases of other teachers' efforts to integrate technology in their teaching, you may be wondering how you might go about developing your own technologically supported and curriculum-based lessons, projects, and units. As you know, TPACK is the knowledge that helps teachers to do this successfully. It represents teachers' practical knowledge of curriculum, pedagogy, technology, and teaching/learning contexts that supports integrating technology into their practice and their students' learning. One way to begin to develop TPACK is to explore other teachers' technologically supported curriculum designs. Our hope is that by working through the cases that appeared in previous chapters, you have begun to develop your own TPACK.

TPACK can also be developed during the process of designing your own lessons, units, and projects. This chapter will introduce you to a TPACK-based planning process with learning activity types that you can use to design curriculum-based and student-centered lessons that integrate technology effectively, building your TPACK while doing so. You will maximize your learning from this chapter if you complete all of the phases of the planning process that are described here. Using these steps, by the time you complete this chapter you will have designed a technology-enhanced lesson to use in your classroom. You can then continue to use this process, building your TPACK over time as you design and offer additional learning experiences to your students.

Building Blocks - Learning Activity Types

As you read through the cases, you may have noticed that each lesson or project in the Practitioner's Guide was structured with a combination of different learning activities. What happens during learning activities tends to differ by curriculum area and students' learning levels. Some learning activities are used in multiple curriculum areas; for example, mapping ideas, conducting research, and developing presentations are activities used in nearly every curriculum area. However, even though a learning activity might be used in different curriculums, the way it is interpreted and conducted differs (Stodolsky, 1988). For example, a student-created presentation of common literary themes reflected in a collection of poems is structured quite differently than a presentation documenting the process and results of an experiment done by students in a chemistry class.

Typically, lessons, units, and projects in different curriculum areas comprise learning activities that are more different than similar. You would not likely challenge your students to engage in sentence analysis in a science class or to do computation in an English class. The rich media-infused cases featured in this book are structured primarily with these kinds of discipline-specific learning activity types in mind. For example, the estimation and evaluation of mathematical work learning activities in the Elementary Mathematics case are unique to mathematics. Similarly, creating a timeline and designing an exhibit – both learning activity types included in the social studies cases – would most likely be found in social studies lessons and projects. A review of lesson, project, and unit plans in any curriculum area will quickly reveal the range of different learning activity type possibilities available for teachers to choose among and combine as they structure curriculum-based learning experiences for their students. The ways in which these learning activities are selected, combined, sequenced, and facilitated guide student learning.

Taxonomies of Learning Activity Types

How, though, does a teacher – especially a new teacher – know which types of learning activities are possible within differing curriculum areas? While working with both experienced and novice teachers, we have discovered that it is helpful to know the full range of plausible learning activities in each curriculum area to assist with planning lessons, projects, and units. This knowledge encourages teachers to be creative in the ways in which they design learning experiences, reach a broader range of student learning needs and preferences, and prevent overuse of particular learning activities in their planning, which helps to build and maintain students' engagement.

Experienced teachers tend to identify favorite learning activities that seem to work well for their students and for them. They then may use these particular types of learning activities with greater frequency than others. This kind of "routinization" (as described in Yinger, 1979) is both understandable and efficient for busy teachers. Naturally, we use what works. This practice can, however, cause teachers to miss instructional opportunities. If teachers employ only a small subset of possible learning activities in their classrooms, other effective and engaging approaches may be omitted or forgotten.

While these favorite activity types may work well for some students, they may create unintended and unnecessary barriers for others. The Universal Design for Learning (UDL) framework encourages teachers to consider these learning barriers, planning a variety of learning activities that give students multiple ways to access curriculum content, express their understanding, and engage in the learning process. (Learn more about UDL from Meyer, Rose, & Gordon, 2013). Therefore, the more comprehensive the set of learning activities that exist in a teacher's mental toolbox, the more likely barriers to learning for students with diverse learning styles and preferences will be minimized.

Once we realized that it is helpful and important for teachers to have access to a collection of all possible kinds of learning activities in particular content areas, we began to collaborate with experts in each core curriculum area to develop comprehensive taxonomies of learning activity types (LATs). We purposely chose to develop the taxonomies with as broad a range of LATs as possible – from student centered to teacher centered and everything in between – to provide teachers with as many learning activity options as possible. In this way, we hope to support effective technology integration in every teaching approach, rather than advocate for particular pedagogical styles. To date, we have developed comprehensive taxonomies of LATs in nine different curriculum areas:

- K-6 Literacy
- Mathematics
- Music
- Physical Education
- Science
- Secondary English Language Arts
- Social Studies
- Visual Arts
- World Languages

Each of the LAT taxonomies is organized by key themes or foci in each content area. This organization differs substantially among different content areas. For example, in K-6 Literacy, the LATs are classified first according to the two primary focal areas in English language arts: reading and writing. In mathematics, the taxonomy is subdivided into categories that correspond with the National Council of Teachers of Mathematics (NCTM) Process Standards. In social studies and science, the taxonomies are divided into LATs that encourage knowledge development and knowledge expression. The primary goal of these organizing ideas is to make the taxonomies as intuitive and usable as possible for teachers.

The taxonomies themselves are structured in a table with three columns that offer the name of the LAT, a brief description, and possible technologies that can be used to enhance or support learning and teaching with this type of learning activity. The descriptions are brief so that they can help teachers envision the possibilities of using particular LATs without constraining ideas for adapting the LATs to fit students' needs and preferences. The list of technologies for each activity type is not meant to be comprehensive. Rather, the possibilities included here provide examples of recommended digital tools for teachers to consider using. The following excerpt from the Knowledge Building Activity Types from the Social Studies LAT Taxonomy illustrates the taxonomies' three-column structure.

Table 1

Knowledge Building Activity Types (excerpt)

Activity Type	Brief Description	Possible Technologies
Read Text	Students extract information from textbooks, historical documents, census data, etc.; both print-based and digital formats	Digital archive, Web site, electronic book, audiobook
Read Maps, Charts and Tables	Students extract and/or synthesize information from maps, charts and/or tables	Textbook supplement, Web-based datasets (e.g., CIA World Factbook)
View Presentation	Students gain information from teachers, guest speakers, and peers; synchronous/asynchronous, oral or multimedia	Presentation software, videoconferencing, video creation software (e.g. Movie Maker, iMovie), concept mapping software
View Images	Students examine both still and moving (video, animations) images; print-based or digital format	Presentation software, word processor, video creation software (e.g. Movie Maker, iMovie), image sharing sites (e.g. Flickr.com)
Listen to Audio	Students listen to audiorecordings of speeches, music, radio broadcasts, oral histories, and lectures; digital or non-digital	Digital audio archive, podcast (e.g., "Great Speeches in History," etc.), audiobook

Many teachers and teacher educators have asked us why we don't simply provide a single taxonomy of learning activities that could be used regardless of curriculum area. This would certainly be more efficient – particularly for elementary teachers who teach in multiple curriculum areas. However, a brief examination of some of the taxonomies and how they are subdivided reveals the substantive differences in both activities and taxonomy structure by curriculum area and, therefore, the need to provide separate taxonomies for each. We will illustrate this point with overviews of the structures of six of the taxonomies next.

Literacy and English Language Arts LATs

Educators have also asked us about accommodating grade-level differences in content to be learned and taught using LATs. We considered this suggestion while working with curriculum experts to develop the taxonomies. Based upon their advice, only one curriculum area – language arts – was divided into separate sets of LATs for elementary and secondary teachers. Not surprisingly, these two taxonomies are structured very similarly, as illustrated in Table 2. In each taxonomy, the two primary categories are Reading and Writing. Each of these two categories are subdivided into Pre-, During-, and Post- stages. The K-6 Literacy taxonomy adds two subcategories: Writing Conventions and Writing Genres. The Secondary English Language Arts taxonomy adds three more: Language Focused, Oral Speaking/Performing, and Listening/Watching. These additional categories are necessary in the secondary-level taxonomy due to the complexity and specificity of curriculum expectations in English/language arts at this level.

Table 2

Overview of the K-6 Literacy and Secondary English Language Arts LATs Taxonomies

K-6 Literacy Taxonomy LATs Categories	Secondary English Language Arts Taxonomy LATs Categories
Reading (Pre-Reading, During-Reading, Post-Reading, Vocabulary, Comprehension, Fluency)	Reading (Pre-Reading, During-Reading, Post-Reading)
Writing (Pre-Writing, During-Writing, Post-Writing)	Writing (Pre-Writing, During-Writing, Post-Writing)
Writing Conventions	Language-Focused (Language Exploration, Awareness & Inquiry, Language Composing, Language Analysis, Language Conventions, Vocabulary Development)
Writing Genres	Oral Speaking/Performance
	Listening/Watching

Science and Social Studies LATs

Another two curriculum areas for which taxonomies are structured similarly are [Science] and [Social Studies]. In both of these taxonomies, the primary LAT categories are Knowledge Building and Knowledge Expression. The ways in which these two categories of LATs are subdivided are different. Unlike knowledge building in Social Studies, Science knowledge building is subdivided into Conceptual and Procedural types. In Social Studies, curriculum content is primarily conceptual, so it was not necessary to subdivide the Knowledge Expression LATs. However, the range of ways that students can express their understanding of curriculum concepts in Social Studies is broader than the range of ways students can build conceptual knowledge. Therefore, we subdivided the Social Studies Knowledge Expression LATs into six different subcategories, which are noted in Table 3.

Table 3

Overview of the Science and Social Studies LATs Taxonomies

Science Taxonomy LATs Categories	Social Studies Taxonomy LATs Categories
Conceptual Knowledge Building	Knowledge Building
Procedural Knowledge Building	
Knowledge Expression	Convergent Knowledge Expression
	Written Divergent Knowledge Expression

	Visual Divergent Knowledge Expression
	Conceptual Divergent Knowledge Expression
	Product-Oriented Divergent Knowledge Expression
	Participatory Divergent Knowledge Expression

Mathematics and World Languages LATs

LATs that focus upon process-oriented learning appear in the Mathematics and World Languages taxonomies. The processes are quite different in these two curriculum areas, however, as you might expect. In Mathematics, the LATs are delineated using the NCTM Process Standards. In World Languages, the LATs reflect the American Council on the Teaching of Foreign Languages (ACTFL) Standards for Foreign Language Learning, which emphasize communication skills. These two sets of process-oriented standards—which also organize the mathematics and world languages taxonomies —are summarized in Table 4.

Table 4
Overview of the Mathematics and World Languages LATs Taxonomies

Mathematics Taxonomy LATs Categories	World Languages Taxonomy LATs Categories
Consider Practice Interpret Produce Apply Evaluate Create	Listening Speaking Writing Reading Viewing

These comparisons of LAT taxonomy structures reflect the realities of teaching and learning within and across different curriculum areas as they are practiced in most districts, schools, and classrooms. Although some similarities exist among the structures of the taxonomies and in the LATs included in each curriculum area, more differences than similarities are apparent. These differences in content and teaching practices are why we have created differing taxonomies of learning activities in different curriculum areas.

Identifying and Substituting LATs

How do teachers learn to use LATs to assist their instructional planning? It is helpful to begin by unpacking existing plans for lessons, projects, and units to see how sequences of LATs are combined to create curriculum-based learning experiences. During this process, you can see how the teacher-designer structured the plan and consider also how substituting different LATs might change the nature of the planned learning experience.

Identifying LATs

First, we encourage you to print out a copy of the LAT taxonomy(ies) for the curriculum area(s) in which you are doing instructional planning, and keep the paper copy beside you as you continue to explore the rest of this chapter. All of the taxonomies are available on the LAT website (http://activitytypes.wm.edu) in both interactive and .pdf formats. Read through the introduction to the taxonomy with which you will be working first, reviewing its structure, then consider the LATs that it contains.

Next, go back to one or more teaching cases in this book and try to identify the LATs that are incorporated within each lesson or project, using the relevant taxonomy as a guide. If there are other teachers working with this book at the same time that you are, it might be helpful to discuss the LATs present in particular cases with those colleagues.

Substituting LATs

Then, think about other LATs that could be substituted for the ones that you discerned in one of the cases in this book. Considering alternative LATs for a particular lesson, unit, or project is one of the most powerful ways to utilize the LAT taxonomies. By generating multiple combinations of LATs to address a particular learning goal, you can meet a broader range of student learning needs and preferences (a UDL-based approach) or the specific requirements and predilections of specific students (a differentiation-based approach). The nature and outcomes of a learning experience can be altered dramatically merely by substituting one LAT for another.

For example, in the Secondary Social Studies case, students shared their understanding of a global issue at the end of the project by Developing an Exhibit in the form of a website. This approach enables students to use a variety of digital media to educate their peers and other Web viewers about the issue they selected. Imagine, however, if they were challenged to Engage in Civic Action related to the same global issue at the end of the unit. Students could instead take action related to the issue in a number of ways, which can both enable students to express their understanding (UDL Principle 2) and apply their learning in a real-world application (UDL Principle 3). If students were, for example, to organize a letter-writing campaign to local governmental representatives to encourage action or plan and conduct a public rally in support of a particular cause, they would come away with very different understandings and experiences than they did by creating a website.

Test this LAT substitution process for yourself as you review the TPACK case that you selected and explored. Note that although alternative combinations of LATs will be used to address the same learning goal(s) that were introduced in the case, the new learning experience may be quite different for students.

Explore another case in the same curriculum area as the one you selected earlier. First, identify the LATs that seem to be present in the case, then consider and note alternative possibilities as you did previously. This time, though, consider ways that you could make the learning design either more teacher directed or student centered. Also, consider how you might make the activity more open ended or more scaffolded.

When you view the LATs as interchangeable components in a learning design, they become like building blocks. Just as when children use wooden blocks to build castles of different shapes, sizes, and designs, in altering the building blocks of a lesson or project, you can create entirely different experiences for your students.

By exploring existing combinations of LATs in practice and considering how different LAT choices alter the nature of a lesson or project, you will both build familiarity with the LAT taxonomies in your curriculum area(s) and begin to understand how different combinations and sequences of activity types can assist different types of learning. Once you have built this familiarity, the next step is to use the one or more LAT taxonomies to plan entirely new experiences for your students. In the next section, we will explain how you might select and sequence particular LAT combinations from all of the choices available to you.

Planning with the LAT Taxonomies

We encourage teachers to design learning experiences with the LATs using a flexible five-step process:

1. Choose learning goals.
2. Consider classroom and school contexts.
3. Select activity types to combine and sequence.
4. Select assessment strategies.
5. Select tools and/or resources.

While this process is presented in a linear fashion here, in reality you may choose to reorder the steps (e.g., some teachers prefer to consider assessments earlier in the planning process than depicted here) or plan using a more recursive process. However you approach planning with LAT taxonomies, we recommend always beginning with learning goals and ending with selecting possible tools and resources. In this way, technology use will be grounded in students' curriculum-based learning needs, rather than in the particular features of educational tools or resources. As you work through the following sections, we encourage you to use these steps in a flexible way to design your own technologically enriched learning experiences for your students.

1. Choose Learning Goals

When first learning about using taxonomies of LATs to plan instruction, novice teachers often ask us, "Where do I begin?" and "How do I know which of all these LATs to choose?" These are understandable questions, given the number of possible choices and combinations of LATs. In reality, the answer is clear and always the same: Begin with your students' curriculum-based learning needs. Whether these are suggested by state curriculum standards or a school district's curriculum scope and sequence, it is important to begin planning all learning experiences with student-focused learning goals clearly in mind. Goals for learning can differ from particular curriculum standards, however. When identifying the particular learning goals around which you will structure a lesson, unit, or project you must decide specifically what you hope the students will take away from the learning experience.

✔ Begin by identifying a learning goal from your curriculum upon which you would like to focus a lesson or part of a project. Choose a standard from your state or district curriculum, then describe in writing as clearly as possible what you hope your students will learn by engaging in a learning experience that is designed to address this particular standard.

2. Consider Your Classroom and School Contexts

Once you have identified the learning goals for a particular lesson, project, or unit, you must consider the context of the classroom in which you are teaching (and in many cases, the school, too). Effective instructional plans are not designed for generic classrooms or students. They are designed for a particular classroom context that includes a number of different elements, including

- the physical classroom space,
- the time of day during which the planned learning will take place,
- the degree to which student desks or tables can be rearranged,
- the amount of time available for the learning experience, and
- the digital and non-digital tools and resources available to your students and you.

Of course, teachers also plan with specific students in mind. Specifically, teachers consider student-related variables including the following:

- students' prior knowledge and experience with the focus of the learning experience being planned,
- students' learning preferences (e.g., preferred types of activities and materials),
- the amount and type of structure required for these particular students, and
- collaborative grouping strategies that are most effective for these particular learners.

These contextual realities – and many more – should be considered when determining the optimal combination and sequence of learning activities in a lesson, unit, or project that is being planned.

To prompt your thinking about some of these contextually influenced decisions, we have created the following chart. While experienced teachers consider these types of variables almost automatically when planning instruction, novice teachers may find it helpful to place their design decisions on the continua pictured here as they work through the planning process.

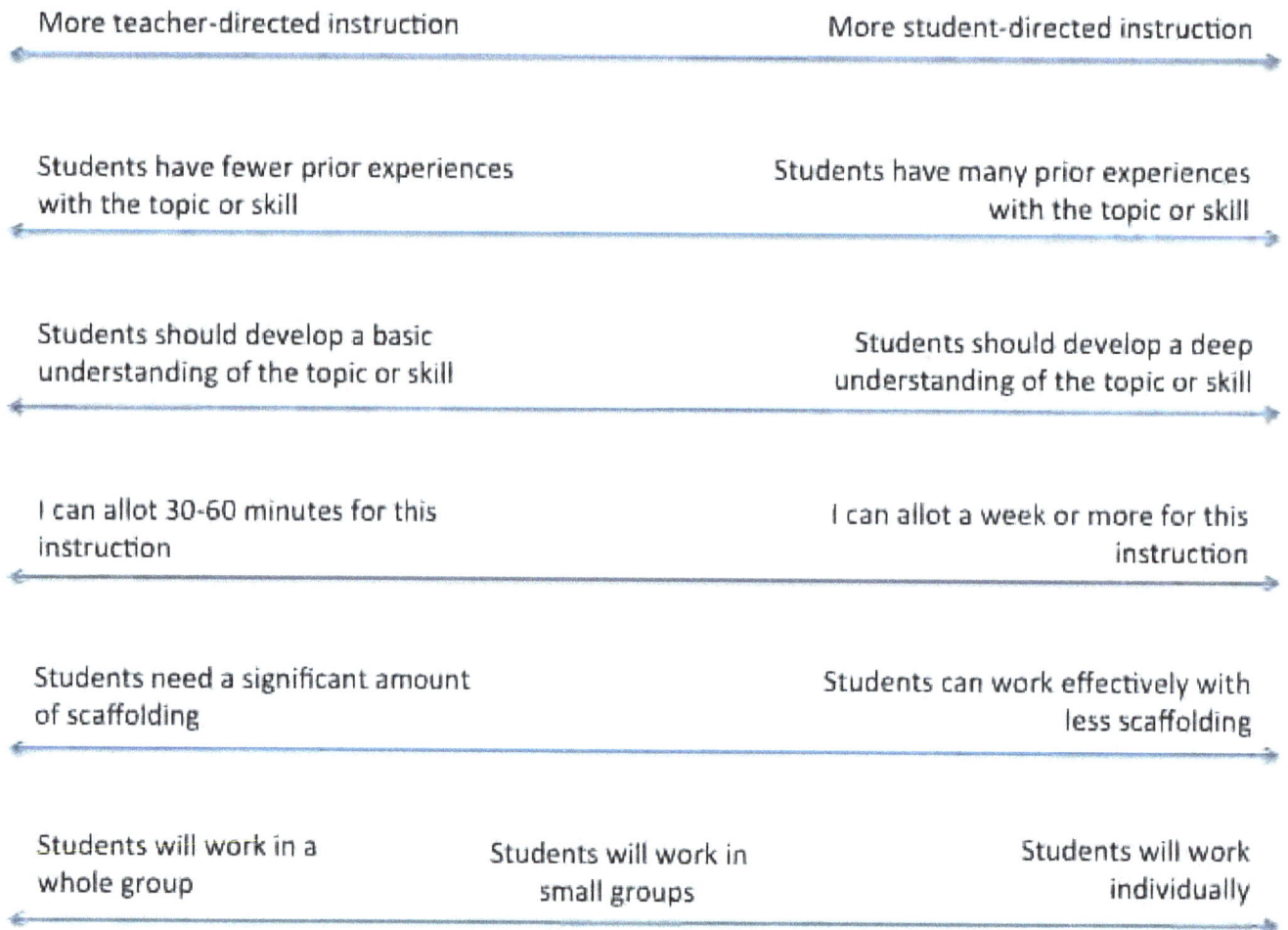

More teacher-directed instruction ←——————————————→ More student-directed instruction

Students have fewer prior experiences with the topic or skill ←——————————————→ Students have many prior experiences with the topic or skill

Students should develop a basic understanding of the topic or skill ←——————————————→ Students should develop a deep understanding of the topic or skill

I can allot 30-60 minutes for this instruction ←——————————————→ I can allot a week or more for this instruction

Students need a significant amount of scaffolding ←——————————————→ Students can work effectively with less scaffolding

Students will work in a whole group ←———— Students will work in small groups ————→ Students will work individually

✓ Now that you have identified learning goals for your lesson or project, think about what you know about the classroom and school in which you will be sharing this learning experience with your students. Choose places on as many of the pedagogical decisions continua as you can that represent your knowledge of the students and their classroom and school contexts. Be as realistic as possible. If you are not able to mark one or more of the continua, leave it blank until you learn more about the students and context in which you will be facilitating the learning experience that you are planning.

3. Select LATs to Combine and Sequence

After determining the learning goals and contextual factors that will help shape the learning experience you are planning, it is time to choose the building blocks for the learning design. The LAT taxonomies present the full range of types of learning activities in each curriculum area from which teachers can choose during instructional planning. Each taxonomy is subdivided into categories of LATs to guide this selection. When designing a reading project or unit for a third-grade classroom, for example, it may be important to consider activity possibilities from each of the stages of the reading process: "pre-reading," "during-reading" and "post-reading." Alternatively, in a World Language classroom, if students are working toward engaging in brief conversations in the target language, it might be helpful to combine and sequence different Listening and Speaking activities to structure that experience.

If you have decided to use a particular pedagogical model or approach in your planning, its characteristics and emphases can guide your selection of LATs. For example, many science teachers utilize some form of a 4 E's learning cycle, which recommends a sequenced lesson structure of engagement, exploration, explanation, and extension. If you intend to use a 4 E's approach in the lesson you are designing, you could consider different LAT possibilities for each of these four phases of the lesson plan before selecting the particular activities that will comprise the lesson.

During earlier stages of planning, consider multiple possible combinations and sequences of LATs. As illustrated earlier, slightly varying combinations of LATs can produce quite different learning experiences for students. It is critical to focus upon the learning goals for the lesson while keeping the contextual factors in your peripheral vision as you consider different LATs to combine and sequence to form the lesson, project, or unit you are planning.

> Complete the LAT Planning Guide (http://editlib.org/go/PlanningGuide) for your lesson or project. Once you have identified a range of possible LAT options, decide upon the optimal combination, then sequence the LATs for your lesson using models and/or strategies that you have learned about in your teaching methods courses.

4. Select Assessment Strategies

Teachers can employ a range of different types of formative and summative assessment activities to monitor, assist, and evaluate student learning. When you hear the word assessment, you may think of different types of summative assessment strategies, for example, quizzes and tests. Summative assessment activities are included in all of the LAT taxonomies.

However, many of the other LATs can be used for either formative or summative assessment purposes. For example, in the K-6 Literacy taxonomy, Retelling, Discussing, and Evaluating activity types can all serve as formative or summative assessment opportunities. In mathematics, almost any of the LATs in the taxonomy can be used either formatively or summatively for assessment of student learning. As you are planning each learning experience, consider one or more ways of monitoring or assessing students' progress in relation to the learning goal(s) for the lesson, unit or project.

> ✓ As you review the LAT sequence that you constructed during the previous planning step, consider what assessment opportunities you have included. If there are limited formative or summative assessment opportunities in your emerging plan, go back to the taxonomy to identify more LATs to add.

5. Select Tools and Resources

You may have noticed very little discussion of technology up to this point in the planning process. While this omission is perhaps unusual in a book designed to explore curriculum-based technology integration, we deliberately chose to wait until this last instructional planning step to consider incorporating technologies. Too often, learning designs can be overly influenced by the features and opportunities provided by specific digital tools and resources without sufficient focus upon the appropriateness of using those particular technologies to help students to meet specific learning goals. It is important to determine learning goals, student needs and preferences, LAT sequence, and assessment opportunities before considering how digital tools and resources might support or enhance the learning experience being planned for students. Once the basic structure and sequence of the lesson, project, or unit have been determined, you can consider suggested tools and resources recommended for use (in the taxonomy) with each of the LATs that comprise your emerging design.

Many of the suggested technologies that appear in the LAT taxonomies are probably familiar to you. For less familiar technologies, links are provided to descriptions and examples in the interactive versions of the taxonomies available on the LAT website (http://activitytypes.wm.edu). An example of this supplementary information appears to the right.

Virtual manipulative, Web-based puzzle (e.g., magic squares), mathematical brainteaser Web site

Virtual Manipulatives Site

Definition

Web-based virtual manipulatives are used by students to explore and understand mathematical concepts in a more concrete way than afforded by textbooks or other static materials.

Features

Mathematics teachers often use physical or concrete manipulatives (e.g., cones, rods, blocks, tiles, etc.) to help students understand mathematics concepts and operations in a more concrete way. Virtual manipulatives mimic these physical manipulatives, but they are freely available online. Sites like the National Library of Virtual Manipulatives provide free access to a range of virtual manipulatives organized by grade level and mathematics topic. In many cases, supporting instructional materials or suggestions are provided as well.

Links

National Library of Virtual Manipulatives

Math Playground

Manipulatives

How might you choose whether to include a particular recommended tool or resource in your lesson plan?

1. Identify which tools are readily available in your classroom or can be borrowed from resources available in your school. There is little value to designing a plan that includes use of a tool that is not available to you or your students.
2. Determine whether the tool is appropriate for your students' use and the learning goals of the lesson or project. If the tool or resource is either too difficult to use or too simplistic, its use may actually diminish the quality of the learning experience for your students.
3. Consider whether the tool or resource adds value to the learning experience. Integrating technology always increases the time required to plan, prepare, and facilitate learning, the complexity of the experience, and the potential for things to go wrong. When you choose to include a tool or resource, its potential benefit should outweigh these additional costs.

When deciding whether to incorporate a particular tool or resource in a lesson, project, or unit, consider the tools listed for the LATs incorporated in the plan both one at a time and collectively. Each tool or resource should add value to the learning experience. Including a technological enhancement to each of the LATs in a lesson may not be a good idea. Instead, consider where and how the use of particular tools and resources would add the most value for students in a particular learning experience. Focus upon these high yield integrations, rather than incorporating technology per se. Remember that choosing not to use a digital tool or resource may be the best option for you and your students, if their learning is assisted just as well or better by using a non-digital tool or resource.

Review the sequence of learning activities (including assessments) that you have selected. Identify possible digital and non-digital technology options for each. Considering the technologies to which you and your students have access and with which you and they have experience (or would like to explore), decide which of the technologies would add the most value to the learning experience you are planning.

· · · Conclusion ·

Our research suggests that using the LATs taxonomies to design technologically enriched lessons, projects, and units during the planning process helps teachers build their curriculum-specific technology integration knowledge (Hofer & Grandgenett, 2012; Hofer & Harris, 2010). Since the LATs are organized by curriculum area and emphasize pedagogies connected uniquely with each discipline, using the LATs for instructional planning is a practical way of building TPACK. Developing TPACK occurs as part of your daily activities, rather than being added to your already overbooked schedule. Also, because recommended educational technologies are listed for each of the learning activities in each curriculum area taxonomy, the LATs approach to instructional planning addresses content, pedagogy, and technology integration in a balanced and authentic way.

Our work with both novice and experienced teachers using LATs for instructional planning also suggests that using the LATs in instructional planning can help you to be even more responsive to your students' learning needs and preferences, while you express your creativity as an instructional designer. You have probably heard that teaching is both an art and a science. Artists (including teachers) are inspired both by what they want to communicate (e.g., the learning goals for a particular learning experience), and the possible ways to communicate (e.g., with particular pedagogical methods and media). Engaging your creativity, along with the planning tools provided here, can help you to design differentiated learning experiences for your students with multiple options for their active engagement, facilitated by savvy use of a full range of digital and non-digital educational technologies. More choices – of both LATs and tools – made available to you as an instructional designer can help you to reach more of your students in ways that are effective for each of them. As you do so, you will be building your professional knowledge – your TPACK – in authentic and pragmatic ways.

References

Hofer, M., & Grandgenett, N (2012). TPACK development in teacher education: A longitudinal study of preservice teachers in a secondary M.A.Ed. program. *Journal of Research on Technology in Education, 45*(1), 83-106. Retrieved from http://digitalcommons.unomaha.edu/tedfacpub/34

Hofer, M., & Harris, J. (2010). Differentiating TPACK development: Using learning activity types with inservice and preservice teachers. In C. D. Maddux, D. Gibson, & B. Dodge (Eds.). Research highlights in technology and teacher education 2010 (pp. 295-302). Chesapeake, VA: Society for Information Technology and Teacher Education.

Meyer, A., Rose, D.H., & Gordon, D. (2013). *Universal design for learning: Theory and practice*. Wakefield, MA: CAST, Inc.

Stodolsky, S. S. (1988). *The subject matters: Classroom activity in math and social studies*. Chicago, IL: The University of Chicago Press.

Yinger, R. (1979). Routines in teacher planning. *Theory into Practice, 18*(3), 163-169.

www.ingramcontent.com/pod-product-compliance
Lightning Source LLC
Chambersburg PA
CBHW081151090426
42736CB00017B/3268